First, Skye Jethani has an epic name. Second, he is brilliant, witty, and deeply biblical. Third, get this book. It will transform your prayer life.

DERWIN L. GRAY Lead Pastor, Transformation Church; author of *God, Do You Hear Me: Discovering the Prayer God Always Answers*

What If Jesus Was Serious . . . about Prayer is creative and convicting, with memorable images rather than formulas or rules. This is a valuable resource that will influence your theology of prayer as well as your practice of it.

KAITLYN SCHIESS author of *The Liturgy of Politics: Spiritual Formation for the Sake of Our Neighbor*

Skye Jethani provides a life-giving reminder that prayer is not reserved for the polished, tidy, and presentable moments of life, but rather, God yearns to be in constant communion with us in our messy, ordinary, everyday lives.

GARY HAUGEN founder and CEO of International Justice Mission

I've read dozens of books on prayer, but Skye Jethani's is now one of my favorites. This practical book left me motivated to pray more and equipped to develop a praying life that can change me, the people closest to me, and even our world.

KARA POWELL Chief of Leadership Formation at Fuller Seminary, Executive Director of the Fuller Youth Institute, and coauthor of *3 Big Questions That Change Every Teenager*

The great gift of Skye is to cut through the muddle of confused thinking around the subject of prayer and focus on the profoundly simple instruction Jesus offers. He combines deep theology with practical and accessible illustrations that are incredibly helpful in getting to the heart of what Jesus taught and modeled. Skye's book will be of great help to those who've always found prayer confusing or boring.

MIKE ERRE pastor, author, and host of the *VOX Podcast*

Popular forms of Christianity are obsessed with teaching us how to live *for* God, but they rarely equip us to live *with* Him. And the key to a radically transformed life *with* God? Prayer. Skye Jethani is back with an eminently accessible, highly useful guide to the kind of Christ-centered life so many young Christians are thirsty for. Highly recommended!

PHIL VISCHER creator of *VeggieTales* and cohost of *The Holy Post* podcast

Skye has done it again. In his winsome blend of engaging stories, perceptive insights, creative sketches, and much-needed challenges, he offers new ways to engage with an ancient—and still incredibly significant—practice and posture of prayer. Jesus certainly was serious about prayer—and Skye communicates that truth in a seriously engaging way.

J.R. BRIGGS author, *The Sacred Overlap: Learning to Live Faithfully in the Space Between*; founder, Kairos Partnerships

Could there be a more important question than, How do we pray? Of course not. Sadly, when most people hear the word "prayer," they only think of asking God for things (one type of prayer). Skye Jethani, in his characteristic flare many of us have come to love, opens up a wider, deeper, more ancient vision of prayer—as the pathway to union with God. I can think of no better book to get you started on your journey.

JOHN MARK COMER pastor of Bridgetown Church and author of *The Ruthless Elimination of Hurry*

Skye Jethani has a refreshingly distinct angle of vision about Jesus and the world. Like the first book in the What If Jesus Was Serious? series, this second one reflects Jethani's careful reading of Scripture, and his commitment to help the reader hear and respond. This is just the kind of provocation and encouragement that should come from taking Jesus—and what He taught and embodied—seriously. Watch out or this will change your life!

MARK LABBERTON president, Fuller Theological Seminary

THE ISSUE OF PRAYER:

WHO? ←

WHAT?

WHEN?

WHERE?

WHY?

HOW?

CONCERNED w/ RESULTS

CONCERNED w/ RELATIONSHIP

**1 IF JESUS WAS SERIOUS...
THEN TO WHOM WE PRAY IS MORE
IMPORTANT THAN HOW WE PRAY.**

JESUS DIDN'T PRAY like most people, and He certainly didn't pray like other religious leaders. In the first century, Jewish prayers were liturgical, usually recitations from Scripture, and spoken in formal Hebrew. Jesus, however, prayed in Aramaic— the informal, common dialect—and He spoke to God with intimate, even casual language.

It was evident to His disciples that Jesus related to God very differently than other rabbis related to Him. Therefore, they asked Him, "Lord, teach us to pray." In response to this request, Jesus told them two parables. One about a neighbor asking for bread in the middle of the night, and the other about a son asking his father for a fish.

We often misread these stories as containing some hidden formula about prayer; a tactic for approaching God in order to receive one's request. Some have even understood these stories to mean we must nag God with our prayers in order to motivate Him to act on our behalf.

Before jumping into the actual meaning of these parables, we must first recognize Jesus' focus. The stories aren't primarily about how to pray, but rather about the person to whom we pray. In other words, these parables are designed to shift our understanding of God, not instruct us about the proper process for praying. Unlike other rabbis and teachers who saw prayers almost like magical incantations—formulaic words designed to control and compel a reluctant God to act—Jesus saw prayer as the intimate connection between a dependent child and a loving parent.

As a result, rather than offering a mechanical process for prayer, Jesus wanted to shift His disciple's vision of God. He knows that how we see our heavenly Father will determine how we commune with Him. Our vision of God defines our practice of prayer. Abraham Joshua Heschel put it this way: "The issue of prayer is not prayer; the issue of prayer is God."[2]

 READ MORE Matthew 6:5–8; Romans 8:15

2 IF JESUS WAS SERIOUS... THEN GOD'S CHARACTER MATTERS MORE THAN OURS.

THE ASSUMPTION IN JESUS' culture was that God's response to prayers depended upon a person's righteousness. Being honorable and upright wins God's favor and He will grant your requests. Most people still think this way about prayer, but Jesus' story about a neighbor asking for bread in the middle of the night challenges this popular assumption.

The story is often misunderstood by modern audiences because we do not recognize the social dynamics at play.

Ancient Israel was an honor-based culture and highly communal. A person's reputation was of paramount importance, and their reputation was inexorably linked to their extended family and community.

Failing to provide bread to an unexpected visitor, which is the core problem in Jesus' story, would not only bring shame upon an individual but also upon the entire village. Therefore, the man with the guest wakes his neighbor in the middle of the night and asks for bread. At first the friend refuses. He is already in bed, but Jesus says, "I tell you, though he will not get up and give him anything because he is his friend, yet because of [*anaideia*] he will rise and give him whatever he needs" (Luke 11:8).

The Greek word *anaideia* is the key to the entire parable, and it's difficult to translate. Some English Bibles say "boldness" or "persistence," leading some to conclude that we must nag God to act on our behalf. This interpretation would mean God is a reluctant provider or disinterested in our needs. That is a terrible misreading.

A more literal translation is "without shame." Jesus is saying that the sleeping neighbor's friendship won't motivate him to get out of bed and help, but his desire to protect his own reputation will. He desires to be honorable and "without shame," and he does not want shame to come upon his community for failing to provide for a visitor. Therefore he will do the right thing.

Jesus' point about prayer is remarkable and simple: God does not answer prayers because of *our* reputation, but because of *His*. Jesus takes the focus off our righteousness or even our relationship with God, and instead emphasizes God's desire to maintain His own honor.

This contradicts virtually every religious impulse, in every person, in every culture. We want to believe that a prayer succeeds or fails because of the person praying—because of a person's holiness, righteousness, or devotion. But Jesus says it's not about us at all. Instead, prayer is received and answered because our heavenly Father is holy and righteous, and because He is devoted to us. We do not have to convince God to act on our behalf, and prayer is not a religious way of nagging God. Prayer, at its most fundamental level, is simply asking God to be God.

 READ MORE **Ezekiel 36:22–23; Psalm 25:4–11**

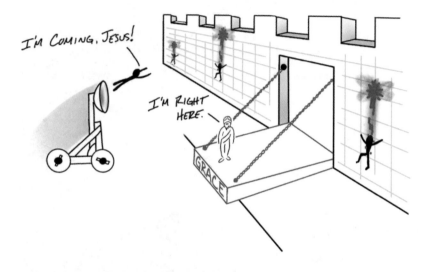

3   IF JESUS WAS SERIOUS... THEN ALL PRAYER DEPENDS ON GRACE.

IMAGINE GOD DWELLING within an impenetrable fortress with walls too high to climb, too thick to penetrate, and too deep to tunnel beneath. Its security is so absolute that not even a signal or message may cross its bulwarks.

Nonetheless, people persist in the belief that they can break through to God. They devise all kinds of elaborate schemes to breach the fortress. *If I just run faster, maybe I can leap over the wall. If I say just the right words, at the right time* and standing in the right spot, maybe the gate will open. If I use the right tool, maybe I can dig through the wall a little each day. Perhaps together we can assemble a great balloon to carry us over the wall! Over time, as each attempt fails, the next one grows more elaborate and more ridiculous.

This metaphor helps explains why human religion is often so odd and extravagant. It also explains why Jesus mocked the prayer rituals common among the pious of ancient Israel. They thought they could breach the fortress and be heard by God because of their eloquence, repetition, strict obedience, or expensive sacrifices. But Jesus knew that is not how prayer works.

Chapter 7 of the Westminster Confession of Faith correctly speaks of the great distance that exists between God and His creatures—a distance too vast for any person to overcome. Our only hope of engaging with God, therefore, is "some voluntary condescension on God's part."[3] In other words, we cannot invade the fortress from the outside, but God can choose to open the gate from the inside.

Applying this truth to prayer, we must understand that our prayers do not reach God because of who we are or anything we do. We possess neither the power nor the righteousness to be heard by Him. Therefore, all prayer relies on God's grace; His unearned hospitality to welcome us into His presence and receive the overflow of our jumbled hearts. Richard Foster put it this way:

> The truth of the matter is, we all come to prayer
> with a tangled mass of motives—altruistic and

selfish, merciful and *hateful, loving* and *bitter.
Frankly, this side of eternity we will* never *unravel
the good from the bad, the pure from the impure.
But what I have come to see is that God is big
enough to receive us with all our mixture. We do
not have to be bright, or pure, or filled with faith, or
anything. That is what grace means, and not only
are we saved by grace, we live by it as well. And we
pray by it.*[4]

READ MORE Matthew 6:5–8; Ecclesiastes 5:1–3

4 STAGES of PRAYER*

① PRAYING AT GOD

 (PRIDE)

② PRAYING TO GOD

 (FAITH)

③ LISTENING TO GOD

 (HOPE)

④ BEING WITH GOD

(LOVE)

* FROM MARK THIBODEAUX, S.J.

4

IF JESUS WAS SERIOUS...
THEN PRAYER IS WHAT WE MUST
DO, NOT JUST WHAT WE OUGHT
TO DO.

ALL PEOPLE PRAY for one of two reasons—either because they *ought* to or because they *must*. The ought-prayers do it because it is the expectation of anyone who takes religion seriously (or who wants to be perceived as taking it seriously). They occasionally turn to God in prayer as if they are doing Him a favor, or perhaps to tone their "spiritual life" the way one gives extra attention to diet and exercise after the holidays. Deep down the ought-prayers suspect their lives would be just fine without prayer.

The must-prayers are very different and are most easily spotted in hospital waiting rooms or recovery groups. They are desperate souls that have had their illusion of control obliterated by the harder realities of life. They pray because they are utterly convinced of their need for God and His grace. Despite what others may conclude from their appearance, the must-prayers know that apart from God's presence their lives would unravel. For them, prayer is not optional.

If ought-prayers see prayer like perfume, a welcome but nonessential addition to the air, then must-prayers see it like oxygen, the element of the atmosphere their life depends upon.

We have all had must-pray moments triggered by acute fear or insecurity, but then we drift back into the ought-pray mindset when our circumstances return to normal and our illusion of control is restored. To cultivate real communion with God, however, we must not lose sight of our dependency and our poverty. If we do not believe we need God, we will not receive Him. As Augustine said, "You must account yourself 'desolate' in this world, however great the prosperity of your lot may be."[5]

 READ MORE Psalm 73:23–26; 1 John 1:5–10

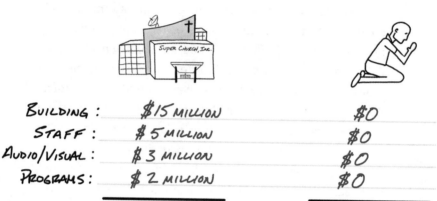

BUILDING :	$15 MILLION	$0
STAFF :	$5 MILLION	$0
AUDIO/VISUAL :	$3 MILLION	$0
PROGRAMS :	$2 MILLION	$0
IMPACT :	DECLINING	INFINITE

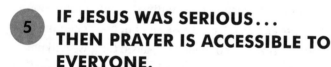

5 IF JESUS WAS SERIOUS... THEN PRAYER IS ACCESSIBLE TO EVERYONE.

A FEW YEARS AGO I was invited to speak at a large trade show where suppliers of theatrical equipment (stage lighting, sound systems, fog machines) showcased their products to church leaders. I was asked to speak about "The Future of Ministry." The event organizers specifically asked me to discuss trends and research related to young adults and how churches could better engage them.

Part of my presentation included a survey that asked

young people, "What has most helped you grow in your faith?" The top response from millennials was "prayer."[6] When I revealed that answer, there was an audible gasp in the room I hadn't anticipated. Sensing the surprise from the audience, I decided to take things a step further. "Do you know what's great about prayer?" I asked the ministry leaders. "It's very affordable." That got a laugh from the crowd, but not from the conference director.

When I came off the main stage he was livid. He explained that the goal of the event was to sell theater equipment to churches so they can create "bigger and better" experiences. My presentation, he said, was not appreciated by the vendors. I explained that I was invited to speak to the pastors not the vendors, and to present data about young adults, not to sell smoke machines. I have not been invited back.

The incident illustrates one of the core dilemmas facing consumer Christianity. It always wants to produce, package, and sell communion with God, but this agenda relies upon people believing communion with God requires some special knowledge or skill they do not possess. If experiencing God's presence requires millions of dollars in theatrical equipment, then I *need* a massive church building and its army of employees to grow in my faith.

But a new generation is discovering a dangerous truth—all the pyrotechnics and hologram projections in the world are no substitute for the simple practice of prayer. And prayer is accessible to anyone, anywhere. As Madame Guyon said, "This way of prayer, this simple relationship to your Lord, is so suited for everyone; it is just as suited for the dull and the ignorant as it is for the well-educated. This prayer, this experience which begins so simply, has as its end a totally abandoned love to the Lord. Only one thing is required—*Love*."[7]

 READ MORE **Matthew 11:25–30; James 4:8**

Different Destinations

Same Departure

6 IF JESUS WAS SERIOUS...
THEN WHAT MAKES CHRISTIAN
PRAYER DIFFERENT?

CHRISTIANS ARE NOT THE ONLY people who have a sense of transcendence in prayer. What some call "mystical" experiences are common across many religious traditions and even in nonreligious practices. Some will say they feel peace and a rejuvenating power in meditation or yoga, or when listening to music. So why should one conclude that Christian prayer is anything more than a universal human capacity for transcendence—with a biblical veneer?

First, we should not dismiss the mystical experiences of those outside the Christian tradition as illegitimate or fabricated. We appear to be creatures hardwired by our Maker for this capacity, regardless of our culture or theology. C. S. Lewis compares mystical experiences to going to sea. Everyone who departs on a voyage has the same essential experience. "The land sinking below the horizon, the gulls dropping behind, the salty breeze. Tourists, merchants, sailors, pirates, missionaries—it's all one."[8] What makes them different is not the experience of leaving the shore, but where they are heading and why they are going.

Similarly, many people report feelings of peace or transcendence produced by any number of practices. This is because, as Lewis puts it, "Departures are all alike; it is the landfall that crowns the voyage."[9] In other words, what differentiates the journey of Christian prayer is not how it begins, but where it ends—in the arms of our heavenly Father.

If we are merely looking for a dose of rejuvenation or a method for relieving stress, any pseudo-religious vessel on any heading will suffice. If, however, we are longing for communion with our Creator, Redeemer, and Healer—then we must take care to embark on the ship that sails to His shore rather than another.

 READ MORE John 14:5–11; Psalm 62:1–2

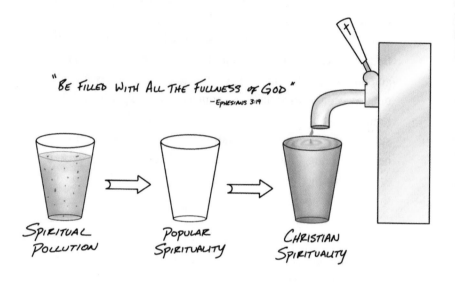

"BE FILLED WITH ALL THE FULLNESS OF GOD"
—Ephesians 3:19

SPIRITUAL POLLUTION   POPULAR SPIRITUALITY   CHRISTIAN SPIRITUALITY

7 IF JESUS WAS SERIOUS... THEN PRAYER IS ABOUT BEING FILLED WITH GOD, NOT JUST EMPTIED OF ANXIETY.

OUR CULTURE IS INCREASINGLY abandoning anything that resembles orthodox Christianity in favor of a generic or sentimental kind of spirituality. This has caused many, including those within the church, to embrace a distorted vision of prayer. They seem to think that prayer is little more than a form of self-therapy but with a spiritual facade. In some places it's seen as a self-improvement practice that any health-obsessed person should do, like working out or eating quinoa.

If you are seeking to develop a discipline of Christian prayer as a kind of soul cleanse that eliminates psychic toxins and emotional cholesterol from your neural pathways, it is best to give up now. Unlike other forms of therapeutic meditation, Christian prayer is not about *emptying* our minds, or *releasing* our burdens, or *replacing* negative thoughts. All of these goals may have some benefit, but their emphasis on emptying sets them in a category altogether different from Christian prayer.

Empty cups are all empty in the same way. Filled cups, however, can be filled with an infinite number of things. To pray like Jesus is to be filled with the presence of God. Henri Nouwen said it this way: "To pray, I think, does not mean to think about God in contrast to thinking about other things, or to spend time with God instead of spending time with other people. Rather, it means to think and live in the presence of God."[10]

Prayer is not an emptying of ourselves or an escape from the world. It is positioning ourselves to be filled with all the fullness of God, and to carry His presence into all we do.

 READ MORE Ephesians 3:14–19; Psalm 42:1–2

LOOKS DOWN

PRAYER

THE DIGNITY OF BEING SEEN

LOOKS UP

8   **IF JESUS WAS SERIOUS...
THEN PRAYER IS ABOUT RELATING
TO GOD, NOT CONTROLLING HIM.**

IF GOD ALREADY KNOWS all things, why do we speak to
Him in prayer? And if our heavenly Father already knows what we
need before we ask Him, as Jesus said in Matthew 6, then why do
we ask Him for anything at all? In other religious traditions with
fallible and capricious gods, it makes sense to pray. In supersti-
tious religions, proclaiming the right words, in the right order
and at the right time, is how one controls deities or provokes
them to act.

The God of Scripture, however, is not fallible, ignorant, or manipulated by any human device, and our prayers do not add to His knowledge in any way. Christian prayer, therefore, is not a means of controlling or informing God, because nothing is hidden from His sight and no one possesses more power.

Still, He invites us to make ourselves and our requests known to Him in prayer, because He desires to relate to us. Through prayer we participate with God and cooperate as persons rather than mere objects of His knowledge.

Consider the story of Peter and John entering the temple in Acts 3. There was a lame beggar at the gate asking for alms. Over the years the man had become part of the background scenery, reduced to an object easily ignored by the crowds passing by. Peter knew the man's needs and could have healed him immediately, but first Peter said to him, "Look at us" (Acts 3:4). The man lifted his head and fixed his eyes on Peter and John. By looking at the apostles he related to them as a fellow man, and they met his need for healing as a person rather than as a project.

Our Lord sees our needs and He can meet them without our prayers, but He longs to give us something more. He wants to give us Himself. Through prayer, as C. S. Lewis says, "we assume the high rank of persons before Him. And he, descending, becomes a Person to us."[11] In prayer, we lift our eyes to look upon the face of God and He bestows upon us the unimaginable dignity of looking back.

 READ MORE **Matthew 6:7–8; Acts 3:1–10**

PART 2

KEEP IT SIMPLE
(AND UNCEASING)

"And when you pray, you must not be like the hypocrites. For they love to stand and pray in the synagogues and at the street corners, that they may be seen by others. Truly, I say to you, they have received their reward. But when you pray, go into your room and shut the door and pray to your Father who is in secret. And your Father who sees in secret will reward you.

"And when you pray, do not heap up empty phrases as the Gentiles do, for they think that they will be heard for their many words. Do not be like them, for your Father knows what you need before you ask him."

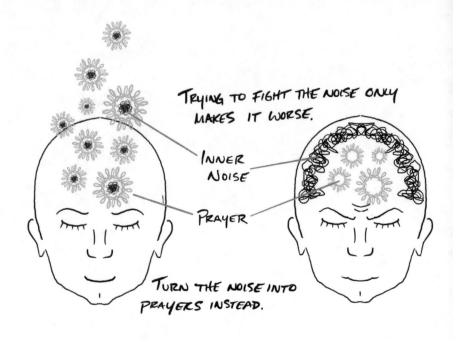

TRYING TO FIGHT THE NOISE ONLY MAKES IT WORSE.

INNER NOISE

PRAYER

TURN THE NOISE INTO PRAYERS INSTEAD.

9 IF JESUS WAS SERIOUS... THEN WE CANNOT WAIT FOR THE NOISE TO STOP BEFORE WE PRAY.

FOR SOME PEOPLE the greatest barrier to prayer is silence. We occupy a very noisy world where we are bombarded by messages competing for our attention. One study estimated that the average American encounters at least three thousand advertisements every day, and that report was done before the creation of smartphones that buzz, beep, and chirp at us incessantly.

Our minds are so accustomed to external stimulation that they go through withdrawal when the noise is turned off. To avoid this pain we replace the need for external distractions with internal ones. Henri Nouwen described it this way: "The trouble is, as soon as you sit and become quiet, you think, *Oh, I forgot this. I should call my friend. Later on I'm going to see him.* Your inner life is like a banana tree filled with monkeys jumping up and down."[12]

What are we to do with our inner monkeys when we are trying to pray? A sure mistake is pretending the monkeys are not there. It only makes them jump and scream more. As someone once said, "No noise is so emphatic as one you are trying not to listen to."[13]

Instead, welcome your monkeys into your prayers. Present to God whatever distracting ideas, tasks, or images flood into your mind. Start praying wherever your thoughts are. If you wait until the monkeys calm down and go away, you'll never pray at all.

 READ MORE **Luke 18:1–8; Philippians 4:6–7**

HOT DOG PRAYER

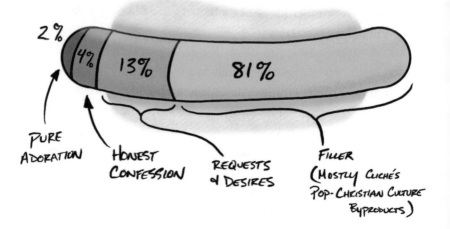

2%

4%

13%

81%

PURE ADORATION

HONEST CONFESSION

REQUESTS & DESIRES

FILLER
(MOSTLY CLICHÉS
POP-CHRISTIAN CULTURE
BYPRODUCTS)

10 IF JESUS WAS SERIOUS... THEN OUR PRAYERS DON'T REQUIRE MANY WORDS.

COMMUNICATION IS EASIER for some people than others. For example, while I enjoy a meaningful conversation as much as the next person, I have little patience for shallow chitchat. Being an introvert, I'd rather enjoy the view out the window than talk about the weather on the other side of it. Others, however, cannot tolerate silence and must fill any verbal vacuum with words.

This same tendency infects our prayers. If we believe prayer is merely talking to God, then to pray more we must talk more. This causes us to pack our prayers with unnecessary filler like a cheap hot dog. Technically it's food, but its nutritional value is questionable. Likewise, when our prayers are filled with details and facts with the goal of informing God, we may be talking *to* Him but are we really communing *with* Him? Our Lord does not listen to your prayers because He is hoping to learn something He did not already know, nor does He need your advice about how to heal Mrs. Jones' arthritis. And He does not need to be reminded to stay on task like a distracted child.

But the omniscience of God raises a valid question. If God already knows everything and we cannot add to His knowledge or wisdom, why do we pray?

First, this question assumes that prayer is primarily about communication, but as we've already seen that is a very narrow and incomplete understanding of prayer. Instead, prayer is primarily about relating to God even when words are not used. When we do employ words, particularly to express our needs to God, we are confessing our dependency upon Him and our lack of faith in ourselves. We are demonstrating our creatureliness and our need for His providence. Unlike hot dog prayers, this can be done with an economy of words. Sometimes it may be as simple as bringing a person or situation to mind, saying, "Lord, have mercy," and then resting in His presence.

 READ MORE **Matthew 6:7–8; Ecclesiastes 5:1–3**

11 IF JESUS WAS SERIOUS...
THEN THE SIMPLEST PRAYERS CAN
LINK EARTH AND ETERNITY.

MANY DON'T KNOW that when Vincent van Gogh was a young man he served as a missionary among coal miners in Belgium. The experience left him with a deep admiration for the working poor. They did not comprehend deep theology, and most did not practice acceptable forms of piety, but they possessed God with a raw authenticity very different from the stiff religiosity van Gogh had known since his childhood.

Vincent produced a charcoal drawing in 1882 that captures his esteem for the coal miners he served. It features an elderly man in a chair near a fire with his face buried in his hard, peasant hands. The reason for the man's posture isn't immediately clear. He could be crying or exhausted, but van Gogh revealed the truth with the drawing's title—*At Eternity's Gate*. It's a portrait of a peasant in prayer. In a letter Vincent wrote, "This is far from theology, simply the fact that the poorest little wood-cutter or peasant on the hearth or miner can have moments of emotion and inspiration which give him a feeling of an eternal home to which he is near."[14]

Van Gogh understood that powerful prayer is available to the ordinary, simple, and even the ignorant. It is for children and peasants, not just the pastors or the powerful. Sometimes we are impressed with those who pray with eloquence or who weave deep theology and Scripture into their petitions to God, and yet the prayer of an unschooled woodcutter asking his heavenly Father for his daily bread can possess the faith to bridge earth and eternity.

We ought to be cautious about seeking "higher" or "more spiritual" forms of prayer, and we ought to be downright suspicious of those promising to teach us special paths unavailable to ordinary Christians. Such ambitions often have little to do with communion with God, and far more to do with elevating ourselves above the spiritual peasants we disdain.

The simple prayer for food, safety, or thanksgiving offered in true dependency is always to be preferred over the elaborate prayer offered in self-righteousness. It's the kind of simple prayer Jesus taught His own disciples. As John Dalrymple said, "We never outgrow this kind of prayer, because we never outgrow the needs which give rise to it."[15]

READ MORE **Matthew 6:1; Matthew 7:7–11**

PRAYER IS...

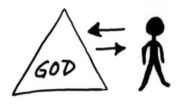

... COMMUNICATION
|
REQUIRES OUR
WORDS

... COMMUNION
|
REQUIRES OUR
HEART, MIND, SOUL, BODY

12 IF JESUS WAS SERIOUS...
THEN PRAYER IS ABOUT
COMMUNION, NOT JUST
COMMUNICATION.

JESUS DID NOT EXPERIENCE union with His Father only
in His moments alone or while praying vocally but also during
His days of active ministry serving, healing, and teaching
others. He spoke of His continual reliance upon His Father's
presence: "the Son can do nothing of his own accord, but only
what he sees the Father doing. For whatever the Father does,

that the Son does likewise" (John 5:19). And Jesus often spoke of living in unity with the Father: "The words that I say to you I do not speak on my own authority, but the Father who dwells in me does his works. Believe me that I am in the Father and the Father is in me" (John 14:10–11).

Prayer as we often understand it, requiring words, did not capture the entirety of Jesus' communion with His Father. The Gospels show us a far deeper, more mysterious, and more intimate connection between the Son and Father that goes beyond words. This wider vision of prayer is often confusing to those who have only understood prayer as communication. For example, CBS News anchor Dan Rather interviewed Mother Teresa in the 1980s and asked her, "When you pray, what do you say to God?"

"I don't say anything," she said. "I listen."

"Well, okay," the veteran journalist tried again. "When God speaks to you, then, what does He say?"

"He doesn't say anything. He listens." Mr. Rather was stumped this time. He had no follow-up question. Mother Teresa simply added, "And if you don't understand that, I can't explain it to you."[16]

Teresa, like Jesus, knew that prayer was communion with God, not just talking to Him. This kind of prayer is what the apostle Paul meant when he called us to "pray without ceasing" (1 Thess. 5:17). Paul wants us to live as Jesus lived—in unending connection with our heavenly Father whether alone or with others, both in silence or with speech.

 READ MORE John 14:8–14; 1 Thessalonians 5:17

49

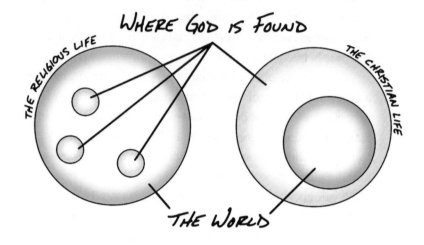

WHERE GOD IS FOUND

THE RELIGIOUS LIFE

THE CHRISTIAN LIFE

THE WORLD

13 IF JESUS WAS SERIOUS...
THEN COMMUNION WITH GOD
CAN BE FOUND ANYWHERE.

NICHOLAS HERMAN was born in 1614 in France. Poverty forced him to join the army for a tiny salary and regular meals. When Nicholas was 18, in the middle of winter, he discovered faith in Christ through a tree. That may sound strange but Scripture is full stories of God using odd things—frogs, donkeys, whales, and even bushes. So a tree is not beyond possibility. The sight of the barren tree sparked Nicholas's imagination. A compiler of his letters wrote about how "he received a high view of the providence and power of GOD . . . and it kindled in him such a love for GOD" that it never faded from his soul.[17] Years later he left the army to enter a monastery, where he changed his name to "Lawrence of the Resurrection."

For the rest of his life, Brother Lawrence served in a kitchen, and it was among the pots and pans that he discovered a peaceful life of continual communion with God. He believed firmly that all work, all places, and indeed all of life was sacred. Going further, Lawrence said those who elevated times of corporate worship as more important, or who used elaborate rituals to drew closer to God suffered from "a great delusion." With words that still challenge our interest in elaborate religious spectacles, Lawrence said:

> *Men invent means and methods of coming at God's love, they learn rules and set up devices to remind them of that love, and it seems like a world of trouble to bring oneself into the consciousness of God's presence. Yet it might be so simple. Is it not quicker and easier just to do our common business wholly for the love of Him?*[18]

Rather than rituals or elaborate church events to fuel his spirituality, Brother Lawrence developed a capacity for ceaseless prayer as the apostle Paul commanded. He conducted his ordinary work in the monastery's kitchen with his mind always attentive to God's presence. He said, "As often as I could, I placed myself as a worshiper before him, fixing my mind upon his holy presence, recalling it when I found it wandering from him. This proved to be an exercise frequently painful, yet I persisted through all difficulties."[19]

Always radiating the joy and tranquility of Christ, Lawrence attracted many others to his simple way of life and prayer. "There is not in the world a kind of life more sweet and delightful, than that of a continual conversation with God; those only can comprehend it who practice and experience it."[20]

 READ MORE **Psalm 139:1–12; Deuteronomy 6:4–9**

PRAYER CHANGES HOW WE SEE

WHAT MOST SEE...

WHAT SOME SEE...

WHAT FEW SEE...

14 IF JESUS WAS SERIOUS...
THEN WE WILL NOT LIMIT PRAYER
TO "SACRED" TIMES OR PLACES.

IN THE OLD TESTAMENT some places were set apart as sacred ground. The most important of these locations was the temple in Jerusalem. It was seen as the point where heaven and earth touched one another. Before the temple, there was Mount Sinai where God Himself descended in billowing smoke and fire to establish a covenant with His people. Sinai was also where Moses first encountered the Lord in the strange sight of a burning bush whose branches were not consumed by the fire. As He drew near, the Lord called to Moses from the bush and told him to remove his sandals because he was walking on holy ground.

The fact that God's presence is more clearly or powerfully experienced in some places is why we still construct ornate, often beautiful spaces for prayer and worship. Because these places inspire our communion with the Lord we should be grateful for them, but we must also be careful not to exaggerate their value. We must not limit our prayers to cathedrals or "sacred" locations. Nor should we foolishly believe our prayers will be amplified because they are offered in this special place rather than that ordinary one.

Moses encountered God through the burning bush on Sinai, but God's presence was not limited to that place. He promised Moses and all of his people, "I will be with you" (Ex. 3:12). And Jesus offered this same promise to His disciples before ascending to the Father. Our God, the Creator and Sustainer of all creation, is not contained by any part of it. All ground is sacred because it all belongs to Him. We merely lack the vision to see it.

So many move through their day blind to the glory of God all around them, but prayer opens our eyes. Some recognize Him only in certain places or at special moments—a worship gathering or maybe in a building they've been told is sacred. The person who learns to commune deeply with God in prayer, however, will open her eyes to see a world bathed in His presence. She will recognize His image in her neighbor and in her enemy, in the sacred and the ordinary, in the intimate and the immense, in the natural and the architectural. She will come to see that every bush burns with His presence.

 READ MORE Exodus 3:1–6; Acts 17:24–29; Isaiah 66:1–2

15 IF JESUS WAS SERIOUS... THEN WE WILL LIVE ON TWO LEVELS AT ONCE.

BY GRANTING US His presence through the Holy Spirit, God has made it possible for us to experience Him in the ordinary reality of our lives. Unlike His people in the Old Testament, we do not have to travel to a sacred site or temple in order to draw near to God. Through His Spirit we may have a constant, unending communion with God. As the apostle Paul commanded, we can "pray without ceasing" (1 Thess. 5:17).

Thomas Kelly called this kind of life with unending

awareness of God's presence as "simultaneity." It's the ability to be engaged with two things at the same time. He described it this way:

> There is a way of ordering our mental life on more than one level at once. On one level, we may be thinking, discussing, seeing, calculating, meeting all the demands of external affairs. But deep within, behind the scenes, at a profounder level, we may also be in prayer and adoration, song and worship and a gentle receptiveness to divine breathings. The secular world of today values and cultivates only the first level, assured that there is where the real business of mankind is done . . . But [we] know that the deep level of prayer . . . is the the most important thing in the world. It is at this deep level that the real business of life is determined.[21]

Take a moment to think ahead to the tasks you have planned today. Invite God to join you in each of them, and consider how you can be reminded of His presence during the day. How can you begin to order your mind on more than one level so you don't miss the real business of life?

 READ MORE **1 Chronicles 16:8-13; Psalm 16:5–11**

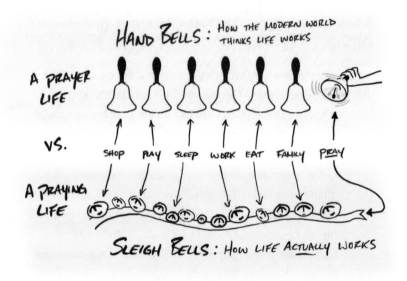

HAND BELLS: HOW THE MODERN WORLD THINKS LIFE WORKS

A PRAYER LIFE

VS.

SHOP PLAY SLEEP WORK EAT FAMILY PRAY

A PRAYING LIFE

SLEIGH BELLS: HOW LIFE ACTUALLY WORKS

16 IF JESUS WAS SERIOUS... THEN WE WILL PURSUE A PRAYING LIFE, NOT JUST A PRAYER LIFE.

MODERNITY HAS GIVEN US many wonderful things like GPS, antibiotics, and instant ramen noodles. It has also given us some less helpful things—including a tendency to separate our lives into disconnected categories. Rather than viewing our life as an integrated whole, we label activities as being part of our "family life" or "work life" or "spiritual life," as if what occurs in one category is distinct and unaffected by what happens in another.

This is largely to blame for our struggles with prayer. Too

many of us think of prayer as something we must add on to our already full schedules, like going to the gym or doing our taxes. Dallas Willard offers a different perspective based on a more integrated vision of life:

> *Don't seek to develop a prayer life—seek a praying life.*
> *A 'prayer life' is a segmented time for prayer. You'll end*
> *feeling guilty that you don't spend more time in prayer.*
> *Eventually you'll probably feel defeated and give up. A*
> *'praying life' is a life that is saturated with prayerfulness—*
> *you seek to do all that you do with the Lord.*[22]

There's certainly nothing wrong with setting aside time for prayer, but this is not the ultimate goal for the Christian. Instead, we are to integrate our communion with God into all that we do and into every moment of our day, and this integrated vision of prayer better fits the way life actually works.

Someone once told me that modern people see life as a set of handbells. Each activity is a separate bell to be rung independently from the others. In truth, life is never that compartmentalized. We are more like a string of sleigh bells that are interconnected. Ringing one bell will automatically affect all of the others.

Try incorporating prayer into each part of your day. When you begin a new task, briefly pause to remember God's presence with you. With or without words, simply invite Him into the life you are already living.

 READ MORE John 5:19–20; 1 Corinthians 7:17–24

PART 3

IT'S OFF TO WORK (WITH GOD) WE GO

"I am the true vine, and my Father is the vinedresser. Every branch in me that does not bear fruit he takes away, and every branch that does bear fruit he prunes, that it may bear more fruit. Already you are clean because of the word that I have spoken to you. Abide in me, and I in you. As the branch cannot bear fruit by itself, unless it abides in the vine, neither can you, unless you abide in me. I am the vine; you are the branches. Whoever abides in me and I in him, he it is that bears much fruit, for apart from me you can do nothing. If anyone does not abide in me he is thrown away like a branch and withers; and the branches are gathered, thrown into the fire, and burned. If you abide in me, and my words abide in you, ask whatever you wish, and it will be done for you. By this my Father is glorified, that you bear much fruit and so prove to be my disciples. As the Father has loved me, so have I loved you. Abide in my love. If you keep my commandments, you will abide in my love, just as I have kept my Father's commandments and abide in his love. These things I have spoken to you, that my joy may be in you, and that your joy may be full."

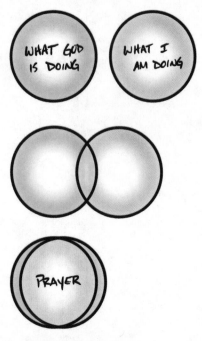

17 IF JESUS WAS SERIOUS... THEN THE LINE BETWEEN GOD'S WORK AND OURS WILL DISAPPEAR.

IN THE LAST SECTION we looked at the difference between a "prayer life" and a "praying life." The former is an activity that we wedge into our busy schedules. The latter is about incorporating prayer into the life we are already living. Dallas Willard goes on to describe the praying life as one of co-laboring with God. He says: "Prayer is talking with God about what we're thinking and doing together; it is co-laboring with God to accomplish the good purposes of His kingdom."[23]

In a real sense, prayer is both how God welcomes us into what He is doing and how we welcome God into what we are doing. As we grow in this practice, the line between His work and ours will becoming increasingly fuzzy until the difference no longer matters. Even labels like *sacred* and *secular*, *ministry* and *vocation*, and *clergy* and *laity* will become nonsensical to us as prayer becomes the lens through which we see all things.

This life-with-God approach to prayer was practiced by Billy Graham. When Graham arrived at the NBC studio in New York for a live television interview on the *Today* show in 1982, one of the producers told his assistant that a private space had been arranged for the world-famous evangelist so he could pray before the broadcast. It was a kind and thoughtful gesture, the assistant said, but he informed the producer the prayer space would not be needed.

The NBC producer was surprised. Maybe he thought Billy Graham wasn't the spiritual giant the country thought he was. Wasn't prayer important before a live national interview? Graham's assistant responded, "Mr. Graham started praying when he got up this morning, he prayed while eating breakfast, he prayed on the way over here in the car they sent for us, and he'll probably be praying all through the interview."[24]

What work has God called you to engage today? Imagine doing that work together with Him in prayer.

 READ MORE **1 Corinthians 3:5–9; Acts 1:4–8**

"THE DIGNITY OF BEING CAUSES"

PRAYER

18 IF JESUS WAS SERIOUS... THEN WE HAVE THE DIGNITY OF BEING CAUSES.

IN THE CREATION STORY we read that God involved the man in His creative work by allowing him to name the animals. As His image-bearer and representative on the earth, the man was granted the dignity of co-laboring with God—a privilege given to no other creature.

Similarly, throughout the biblical narrative we see examples of the Lord involving humans in activities He could easily —and more effectively—accomplish alone. Did He really need

Moses to "let my people go"? Was it necessary for Ezekiel to prophesy over the valley of dry bones in order for God to raise them up? Did Jesus require the participation of fishermen, tax collectors, and other ne'er-do-wells to spread the announcement of His kingdom? If our Lord can cause stones to cry out in worship (Luke 19:40), surely He does not need a blockhead like me to accomplish His purposes.

For His own reasons, however, it has delighted God to do His work, at least in part, through us and with us. Blaise Pascal said, "God has instituted prayer so as to confer upon his creatures the dignity of being causes."[25] This is a wonderful thought—that we are not merely passive stage props in a prewritten cosmic drama, but we are creative partners with God in the writing, directing, design, and action that occurs on the stage of history.

For that reason, prayer is much more than asking God for one thing or another. It is partnering with Him by drawing into deep communion with His Spirit, and in that intimate union taking up our special vocation as His people. In prayer, we are invited to join Him in directing the course of His world.

 READ MORE Genesis 2:18–20; Acts 1:4–8

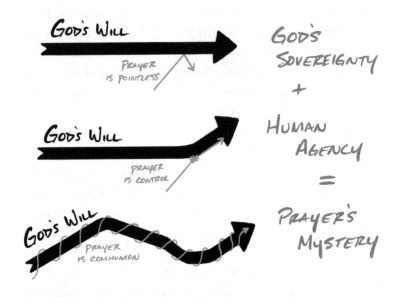

19 IF JESUS WAS SERIOUS... THEN HOW DO OUR PRAYERS CHANGE GOD'S ACTIONS?

IF GOD IS ALL-KNOWING, all-powerful, and unchanging, what real influence can our prayers possibly have on Him? In other words, can our prayers really change God's mind? That's the dilemma some people have with the very idea of prayer, let alone practicing it. It touches on the larger paradox of God's sovereignty and human agency.

While this is a fascinating philosophical question that might keep seminary students debating matters of predestination and free will, it is not a problem recognized by Scripture. Our modern minds get snagged on an either/or scenario—*either* our prayers change God and He is not immutable, *or* they don't change God and prayer is pointless.

The ancient authors of the Bible, however, saw it differently. While modern minds frame the issue as either/or, ancients were more comfortable with the mystery of both/and. For example, the apostle Paul says we ought to "work out your own salvation with fear and trembling, for it is God who works in you" (Phil. 2:12–13). Our modern way of thinking wants to reply, "Wait, Paul. Who is doing the work? Is it me or God?" But that isn't a question he is the least bit interested in answering, because it isn't a question a pre-modern person would ask.

The same indifference applies to prayer. Scripture rejects our question, "Is God sovereign *or* do our prayers make a difference?" and instead affirms that God *is* sovereign *and* our prayers make a difference. How does this work exactly? I haven't a clue. What I do know is that God desires to manifest Himself and His reign over the world through us and with us.

We are called to co-labor with Him, and we are invited— even commanded—to make our requests known to God in prayer. Prayer is how the co-laboring of God and humanity happens. In a mystery beyond my understanding, our will and God's will are mingled just as His Spirit and our spirit abide together in the stillness of prayer.

 READ MORE **Philippians 2:12–13; Romans 8:26–27**

UPWARD PRAYER

NEEDS
THANKS
CONFESSION

POWER
GRACE
AUTHORITY

DOWNWARD PRAYER

20   IF JESUS WAS SERIOUS... THEN PRAYER BRINGS HEAVEN'S POWER TO EARTH.

PRAYER IS HOW MERE mortals present themselves and their needs to the eternal Creator. That is why we usually think of prayers rising up to the higher realm where God abides. Prayers move upward from earth to heaven. But Scripture reveals another dimension to prayer. Ole Hallesby said, "Prayer is the conduit through which power from heaven is brought to earth."[26] In other words, prayer can also move downward.

In common upward prayer, we lift our desires, concerns,

needs, and confessions to God. Downward prayer, which is much less common but shouldn't be, means calling upon the resources available to us in the heavens. If that idea sounds strange to you, it may be because we teach about Jesus' death and resurrection but often ignore His ascension.

The apostles tell us that after Jesus rose from the dead, He spent time with His followers teaching them the meaning of His death and resurrection. After those weeks He then ascended to the right hand of the Father who "has put all things in subjection under his feet" (1 Cor. 15:27). This is royal language that would have been familiar to ancient people. It is the language of a king taking his throne and exercising dominion over his kingdom. When the Bible says Jesus ascended it means that He has started to rule over the world.

But the apostle Paul goes a step further. He writes in Ephesians about those who have been redeemed. He has "raised us up with him and seated us with him in the heavenly places" (Eph. 2:6). And He has blessed us in Christ "with every spiritual blessing in the heavenly places" (Eph. 1:3). This is Paul's way of saying that the power, authority, and resources of heaven accessible to Jesus as He rules over the world are also available to us because we are "in him."

Dallas Willard said it this way, "The treasure we have in heaven is also something very much available to us now. We can and should draw upon it as needed, for it is nothing less than God Himself and the wonderful society of His kingdom even now interwoven in my life."[27]

Downward prayer means to draw upon the power of heaven to see God's will done on earth as it is in heaven. In other words, our prayers carry more authority than we've been led to believe.

 READ MORE Ephesians 1:15–2:7; Hebrews 12:22–24

APOSTLES
PREACHERS
CHURCH LEADERS

"WHOEVER DOES NOT RECEIVE THE KINGDOM OF GOD LIKE A CHILD SHALL NOT ENTER IT."
— LUKE 18:17

FAITH

CHILD

21 IF JESUS WAS SERIOUS... THEN GOD HEARS AND ANSWERS OUR PRAYERS.

KING HEROD HAD ALREADY executed James for preaching about Jesus and His resurrection. Another disciple, Stephen, had been stoned to death by an angry mob. Then in Acts 12, we find the apostle Peter also imprisoned for his refusal to stop preaching about Jesus and likely facing death. In response, the church was earnestly praying for Peter's release.

As they prayed, an angel appeared to Peter in his prison cell. The apostle thought he was dreaming. It was not until the angel opened his cell, led him to the street, and disappeared, that Peter realized his miraculous deliverance was real. He ran through the darkness to the house where the church was secretly gathered in prayer. Rhoda, a young servant girl, heard Peter's voice through the door. She excitedly interrupted the prayer meeting.

"Peter is at the door!" she announced.

"You are out of your mind!" they told her (Acts 12:15). But Rhoda kept insisting it was really Peter. Ironically, the adults stubbornly refused to believe her even as they continued to pray for Peter's release.

The story teaches us something important about prayer. Not a single adult in the story had the faith to believe their prayers for Peter's deliverance had been answered. Not even Peter! He thought the angel freeing him was just a dream. Only Rhoda, a child, believed God had answered their prayers, and her belief came without even seeing Peter. She merely heard his voice through the door.

It isn't enough to pray in desperation. We must also pray in faith—and very often the faith of a child is more than enough.

 READ MORE Acts 12:5–12; James 1:5–8

$$PRAYER > ACTION = PASSIVITY$$

$$PRAYER < ACTION = PRIDE$$

$$PRAYER + ACTION = POWER$$

22 IF JESUS WAS SERIOUS... THEN WE MUST KNOW WHEN TO STOP PRAYING.

WHILE PETER WAS IN PRISON awaiting execution, the church was gathered in Jerusalem to offer "earnest prayer" for him (Acts 12:5). The strange story says that an angel appeared and released Peter in the middle of the night. But when Peter arrived at the home where the church was secretly praying, no one other than a young servant girl believed he was at the door. The adults, still fervently praying, told her she was crazy.

Scripture repeatedly calls us to pray, to appeal to God

with our needs, and to seek His favor for both our friends and our enemies. This is exactly what the believers in Jerusalem were obediently doing for Peter. Scripture, however, does not call us to *only* pray. We must also discern when the time for intercession has ended and we are called to move on.

There is a time for prayer, and there is a time for action. There is a time to cry out to God, and there is a time to claim His victory. There is a time to seek His intervention, and a time to accept His answer. There is a time to ask for His wisdom, and a time to simply obey His command. There is a time to be on our knees, and a time to get up and open the door.

Our failure to discern these moments arises from a popular view that falsely equates prayer with piety and action with its absence. The critical issue is not whether we pray or act, but whether we pray or act *in faith*. The prayers of a thousand priests, prophets, pastors, or preachers are meaningless if they are offered without faith. Conversely, the smallest act of a pagan can move mountains if the pagan acts with faith in Christ.

I wonder how many times, like the Christians in Jerusalem, I have failed to see God's goodness because I could not discern when to stop praying and open the door.

 READ MORE **Acts 12:5–16; Ecclesiastes 3:1–8**

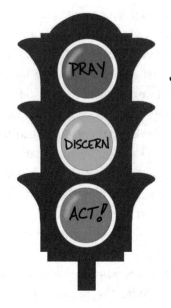

"FOR EVERYTHING THERE IS A SEASON."
—Ecclesiastes 3:1

23   IF JESUS WAS SERIOUS... THEN SOMETIMES OBEDIENCE MEANS NOT PRAYING.

YEARS AGO I WAS TOLD about a consultant hired to help a congregation struggling to raise funds to update and repair their property. After he was introduced at the church meeting, the consultant was invited to pray for the giving campaign.

"I won't pray because we don't have to," he announced to the congregation. "God has already provided all of the money necessary for your property." The members and leaders of the church were confused. The consultant explained that he'd walked through the church parking lot before the meeting and noticed a large number of expensive vehicles. "It's clear God has already given you the wealth," he said. "You just have to use it differently."

Although we assume faith means calling out to our heavenly Father for help, sometimes obedience means *not* praying. Sometimes mature faith means acting with the authority and resources He's already granted us as His beloved children.

Consider the remarkable story of Moses and the Israelites fleeing from Pharaoh's army. The people were trapped by the sea on the east, with the full might of Egypt's soldiers, chariots, and horses bearing down on them from the west. In their terror, "the people of Israel cried out to the LORD" (Ex. 14:10). This phrase echoes back to Exodus 3 when the Lord first appeared to Moses after hearing the cries of His people suffering in slavery. At that time, God said "I have come down to deliver them" (Ex. 3:8). He then commissioned Moses by granting him authority and power to rescue His people.

This time, with the people trapped between the sea and Pharaoh's army, the Lord responded differently to their cries. He said to Moses, "Why do you cry to me? Tell the people of Israel to go forward. Lift up your staff, and stretch out your hand over the sea and divide it" (Ex. 14:15–16). In other words, the Lord told Moses to stop praying and start acting. *I have already given you the power and authority necessary to deliver the people. Now do it!*

 READ MORE **Exodus 14:10–16, 21–22; Mark 11:23**

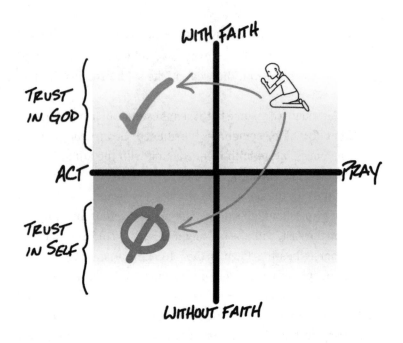

WITH FAITH

TRUST IN GOD

ACT — — PRAY

TRUST IN SELF

Ø

WITHOUT FAITH

24   IF JESUS WAS SERIOUS...
THEN PRAYER IS NOT OPPOSED TO ACTION.

THERE IS AN OLD JOKE about a religious man trapped in his house during a flood who prayed for God to deliver him. A neighbor came to his door offering to drive him away in his truck. "No thank you," the man said, "I trust God will save me." Sometime later the water had reached the second floor of the house. A police boat came to the man's window to rescue him. "No thanks," he said. "I believe God will save me." Eventually, the man was standing on his roof when a Coast Guard helicopter appeared overhead. The man denied their help too and finally drowned in the flood.

In heaven, the man confronted the Lord. "Why didn't you save me?" he asked.

God replied, "I sent you a truck, a boat, and a helicopter. What more did you expect?"

The silly story illustrates a common error. Too often we separate God's actions from our own. We assume God's intervention requires our passivity, and we think taking action ourselves reveals a lack of faith in God's providence. In Acts 25, Paul doesn't make these artificial distinctions.

Earlier in Acts, Jesus had appeared to Paul in a vision, assuring him that he would live to proclaim His gospel in Rome (Acts 23:11). It was a word of encouragement given to Paul while in dire circumstances, but after receiving this promise from the Lord nothing seemed to happen. *Two years* passed as Paul languished away in jail in Caesarea—nowhere near Rome. Finally, when a new governor was appointed, Paul's case came up for review. While standing before the governor, Paul saw his opportunity to get himself to Rome. "I appeal to Caesar," he said. The governor replied, "To Caesar you have appealed; to Caesar you shall go" (Acts 25:12).

Was Paul displaying a lack of faith by getting himself to Rome in this way? Should he have remained silent and waited until God somehow got him there instead? Of course not. Paul fully believed the Lord's promise that he would preach in Rome, but that didn't stop Paul from recognizing—and exploiting— opportunities to get there as they presented themselves. Rather than passively waiting for God, Paul was actively looking for how God might fulfill His promise and then cooperated with Him toward that goal.

Prayer is not opposed to action. In fact, when we act in cooperation with God our actions become a form of prayer that is pleasing to Him.

READ MORE **Acts 25:1–12; 1 Corinthians 15:9–10**

25 IF JESUS WAS SERIOUS...
THEN WE MUST BE CAREFUL NOT TO
ABUSE OUR AUTHORITY.

MANY CHRISTIAN COMMUNITIES and traditions avoid any discussion of authoritative prayer, and when Christians do encounter this under-taught topic they are understandably suspicious. No doubt this is because authoritative prayer has a long history of abuse and manipulation. Huckster preachers on television have employed a perverse form of authoritative prayer to sell desperate people simple solutions. If you just "name it and claim it," they say, all of life's problems will disappear and all the world's blessings will flow your way.

Others have misused authoritative prayer by detaching it from biblical wisdom and surrender to God's will. For example, consumerism has largely obscured any vision for redemptive suffering, and Christians in such cultures can falsely conclude that all suffering is contrary to God's will. When pain or struggle does arise, they employ authoritative prayer to denounce it or the evil forces assumed to be causing it. If the suffering persists, the Christian is left to conclude that her weak faith must be at fault. This only compounds the suffering with the weight of one's own failure.

Finally, authoritative prayer can cause harm when it is linked to what theologians call an "over-realized eschatology." That's a fancy way of describing those who believe the fullness of God's kingdom is already here, and believe that evil, suffering, and injustice have already been fully defeated. Such Christians assume their life with God should be an unbroken sequence of victories. It's a vision of following Jesus that is all resurrection and no crucifixion.

In truth, proper engagement with authoritative prayer requires great maturity and wisdom. It means developing an intimacy with God that produces knowledge of His will. It means discerning when to tell a mountain to move, and when the Lord is calling you to accept the mountain by painfully climbing its cliffs.

 READ MORE **Mark 11:20–25; 1 Timothy 4:1–5**

PETER

JAMES

PRAYERS OF THE CHURCH

FREED

KILLED
RIP

26
IF JESUS WAS SERIOUS...
THEN WE WILL CARE MORE ABOUT BEING FAITHFUL THAN BEING RESPECTED.

AFTER JESUS SPOKE TO THE crowds in Galilee, we are told the people were astonished because "he was teaching them as one who had authority, and not as their scribes" (Matt. 7:29). Jesus carried this authority beyond His teaching ministry. He also banished spirits, healed the sick, lame, blind, and deaf, and He confronted religious leaders with the same authority. That may not be very surprising if we have come to recognize Jesus as God incarnate, but we can often overlook that Jesus also gave His followers "power and authority" to proclaim the kingdom and to heal. This is the basis for authoritative prayer—so why do we rarely use it?

We've already looked at how authoritative prayer is often misused by the immature or abused by spiritual charlatans, but these common perversions aren't the only reasons we ignore authoritative prayer. We also fear if a bold prayer for healing, deliverance, victory, or power goes unanswered, we will look silly and our faith will appear impotent. Related to this fear is a concern for propriety and respectability. Some associate authoritative prayer with ignorant superstition and expressions of religion driven more by emotion than intellect. We'd rather not be associated with those lower forms of faith.

To overcome these fears we ought to remember two things. First, we do not pray authoritatively because our prayers always accomplish what we intend. Instead, we pray authoritatively because we are God's children who have been granted access to His power through Christ's redemption on the cross.

In Acts 12, both James and Peter were imprisoned by King Herod but they experienced very different outcomes. An angel miraculously freed Peter but James was executed. Why did God answer the church's prayers for one apostle but not the other? The important part to remember is that God's purpose was accomplished through both outcomes. Our unanswered prayer, or receiving an answer we do not want, is no reason to neglect the authority granted to us as God's beloved children to make our desires known to Him.

Second, if we fear losing our religious respectability, we ought to remember that neither Jesus nor His apostles were respected by the religious authorities, either. They associated with the wrong people, fasted too little, and failed to observe many of the pious customs of their culture. Jesus and His apostles were far more interested in delivering the oppressed from their chains than winning the approval of their oppressors.

 READ MORE **Luke 9:1–6; Acts 12:1–11**

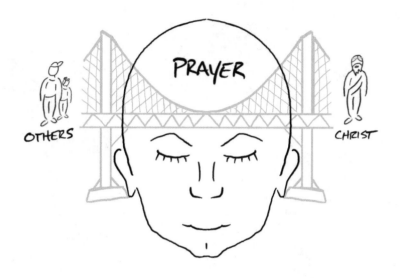

OTHERS · PRAYER · CHRIST

27   IF JESUS WAS SERIOUS... THEN PRAYER IS HOW WE CONNECT OTHERS TO GOD.

JESUS TAUGHT US THAT the two greatest commandments are to love God and to love one another. These commands are fulfilled, at least in part, through prayer. We've already seen how prayer is more than communication *to* God. It is also deep communion *with* God, but this is not its only purpose. As Evelyn Underhill said, "The energy of prayer must be directed on the one hand toward God; and on the other toward people."[28]

When we pray for someone else we are exercising our

priestly calling as an image-bearer of God. In any religious tradition, a priest is someone who stands between another and God to serve as a mediator. A priest is a bridge joining the human to the divine. While we often see the priesthood as a special vocation only a few individuals may practice, it was not always this way. In the beginning, the Lord created all people in His image to be the bridge between Himself and the rest of creation. We were *all* created to be priests.

In prayer we have the great privilege to re-engage our original purpose, which was abandoned when we rebelled against God to pursue our own desires. As we pray we are functioning as a bridge connecting God to His creation and connecting others who need God to His healing presence. Through Christ, we once again get to stand as a conduit between a broken, hurting world and the Lord who is actively redeeming it.

In this priestly position, the two greatest commandments are fulfilled in a single act. First, we actively love the person we are praying for by carrying him into God's presence, which is the greatest good we can ever do for another. Second, we are loving our Lord by expressing our dependence upon Him as well as our trust in His character.

 READ MORE Matthew 18:18–20; 1 Timothy 2:1–6

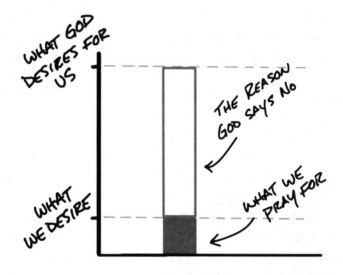

28 IF JESUS WAS SERIOUS...
THEN SOMETIMES GOD LOVES US
TOO MUCH TO SAY YES.

IMAGINE THE DISASTER your life would be if God granted every silly thing you asked for in prayer. That does not mean it is wrong to ask, just as it is not wrong for my eleven-year-old to ask if she may drive my car. But when our Lord says no to our prayers, like a caring father, it is always because He loves us too much to say yes.

While in New Delhi many years ago with my father, a homeless boy begging for money approached us as we tried to cross a busy street. He was rail thin, almost naked, and his legs were contorted upon themselves, yet he was surprisingly fast as he swung on his hands and kneecaps over the broken sidewalk. The boy shouted at us. "One rupee, please! One rupee!" Unable to outpace him, my father finally stopped.

"How about I give you five rupees?" he said. The boy was not amused. He pulled back his hand and gave a dirty look. He assumed my father was mocking him, joking about so lavish a gift. Who would give five rupees, the boy must have thought, when he only asked for one? He waddled away, dejected and cursing us for our cruelty. Then he suddenly stopped. He heard the sound of coins in my father's pocket. As he looked back, he saw my father was holding up a five-rupee coin and placed the coin in the boy's hand.

This is how I imagine God views us. We are destitute children with no hope apart from His help, but rather than asking our heavenly Father for what we need, rather than daring to hope He would give lavishly to those whom He created and loves, we lower our vision and ask for lesser things. In response to our meager requests, God sometimes, but graciously, says no. It's not because we are seeking too much, but because He knows we are asking for too little. In our foolishness we reject Him. We turn away, cursing Him under our breath for not getting what we asked for.

When our Lord says no to our desires, it is because He wants to give us something far more valuable. He offers us Himself.

 READ MORE Luke 10:38–42; 2 Corinthians 12:8–10

PART 4

LEARNING TO PRAY (LIKE JESUS)

Now Jesus was praying in a certain place, and when he finished, one of his disciples said to him, "Lord, teach us to pray, as John taught his disciples." And he said to them, "When you pray, say:

> *"Father, hallowed be your name.*
> *Your kingdom come.*
> *Give us each day our daily bread,*
> *and forgive us our sins,*
> *for we ourselves forgive everyone who is*
>   *indebted to us.*
> *And lead us not into temptation."*

LUKE 11:1–4

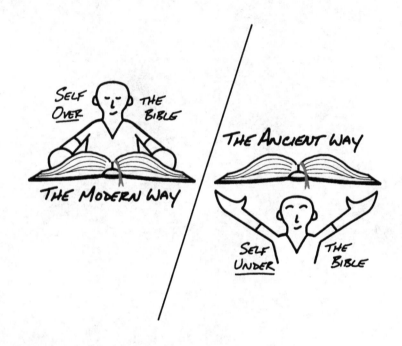

29 IF JESUS WAS SERIOUS...
THEN WE SHOULD USE HIS WORDS
WHEN WE PRAY.

WHEN JESUS' FOLLOWERS wanted to learn how to pray, He taught them to recite His own words. Known as the Lord's Prayer, these verses have guided Christian prayer for two thousand years. The Lord's Prayer points us to the value of using Jesus' words, and all of Scripture, to fuel our communion with God. But to do this we first need to rethink, and possibly unlearn, how we approach the Bible.

Prior to the invention of the printing press in the fifteenth century, most Christians had little or no direct access to the Bible. And even after it was widely available, most were not educated enough to read it. Modern, literate people tend to approach the Bible as a manual or text book—a document to be dissected, mastered, parsed, and implemented. In a manner of speaking, we stand over the text deciding what parts to read, when to read, and how to respond, but this has not been the approach of most Christians throughout history.

While the study of Scripture is certainly a good practice and one more Christians ought to engage in, there is another pre-modern method of engaging the Bible that is better understood as a form of prayer. It's a way of using God's words to fuel our prayers back to Him, and it calls us to humble ourselves under the text as recipients rather than over the text as rulers.

Known by the Latin name *lectio divina*, which means "divine reading," this approach sees the Bible not merely as a collection of principles and applications to grasp, but as the self-revelation of God to His people. It engages the Bible as the living Word of God through which He still speaks and communes with us.

Consider how you've been taught to engage the Bible. Do you see it primarily as a book of answers—a guide to the way to live your best life now? Or, do you engage the Bible as a window through which you see and know God? If the Bible is primarily a manual you'll find its value in prayer to be minimal. If you approach it as a window, however, it may be the most important way you learn to pray.

 READ MORE **Matthew 6:9–13; Colossians 3:15–17**

DIVINE READING

READ
MEDITATE
HOLY BIBLE
CONTEMPLATE
SPEAK

30 IF JESUS WAS SERIOUS... THEN WE SHOULD MEDITATE ON HIS WORDS DAY AND NIGHT.

THE PRACTICE OF divine reading originated in the centuries before copies of the Bible were readily available. Instead, Christians would gather daily at a church or cathedral for the public reading of Scripture. Rather than visually reading text on the page in silence as we do, they received the word audibly as it was read aloud—a model for engaging God's word as ancient as the Scriptures themselves.

Having received and reflected on the Word of God, they

disbanded as each person engaged his or her work for the day. But an individual would retain a word, phrase, or sentence from the Bible reading to foster their communion with God in prayer throughout the day. Eventually this practice was taught in four movements that remain a valuable way to pray today.

Here are the four parts of divine reading as a form of prayer:

1. Read. Gently read the passage of Scripture aloud, being mindful of each word and phrase. The goal is not to read large quantities of Scripture, but to engage it reflectively and with an awareness of God's presence. This may mean reading the text multiple times and then identifying a word or short phrase that speaks to you in some manner.

2. Meditate. In the second movement, allow the Scriptures to read you. Use the passage or phrase to guide your time of reflection and self-examination. How does the passage apply to you and your circumstances? Invite God to speak and reveal what He desires to impart to you through the text.

3. Speak. After allowing God and His Scriptures to have the first word, it is now time for you to respond. Communicate your thoughts to God with words. This may be gratitude, confession, worry, joy, or any number of emotions that result from engaging the Bible.

4. Contemplate. When speaking ceases, it is time to rest in God's presence. Use the remainder of the time to be silent and open to what God has to say. Receive His forgiveness, assurance, or whatever He may have for you.

As you conclude your time with Scripture, take the special word or phrase from the reading with you. Throughout the day you may use it as a prompt for prayer and as a reminder of God's presence with you.

As someone who engages the Bible often as a teacher and writer, I sometimes find it difficult to open Scripture without slipping into an academic or professional posture. I suspect this is a common problem for anyone in ministry, or anyone whose familiarity with the Bible makes a fresh engagement more difficult. This ancient method of divine reading can be a helpful way to break out of that posture and once again commune with God through His Word.

 READ MORE **Psalm 1:1–6; John 5:36–40**

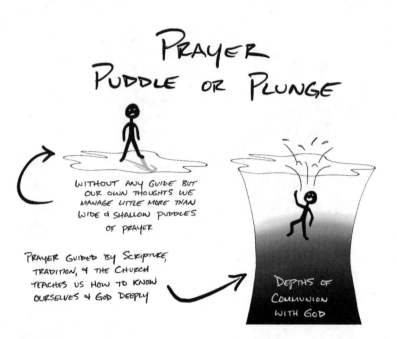

PRAYER
PUDDLE OR PLUNGE

WITHOUT ANY GUIDE BUT
OUR OWN THOUGHTS WE
MANAGE LITTLE MORE THAN
WIDE & SHALLOW PUDDLES
OF PRAYER

PRAYER GUIDED BY SCRIPTURE,
TRADITION, & THE CHURCH
TEACHES US HOW TO KNOW
OURSELVES & GOD DEEPLY

DEPTHS OF
COMMUNION
WITH GOD

31 — IF JESUS WAS SERIOUS...
THEN USING WRITTEN PRAYERS
WILL DEEPEN, NOT CHEAPEN, OUR
COMMUNION WITH GOD.

FOR MANY OF US, prayer is on the very long list of things we *should* do but rarely get around to doing—along with exercising and checking the pressure in our tires. Perhaps after a particularly convicting sermon we decide to be more intentional about setting aside time to pray. We find a quiet place, close our eyes, and then . . . nothing. Our mind wanders in every direction, and when we do manage to formulate coherent thoughts they are little more than empty platitudes and churchy cliches. C. S. Lewis refers to this kind of prayer as "wide and shallow puddles"[29] lacking any real depth or value. If we have this experience with prayer often enough, it's understandable why we abandon the practice or demote it to our "should do" list.

The solution is not to abandon prayer, but to learn how to find the deep, life-giving waters we crave in our communion with God. This is one of the benefits of using written prayers like the Psalms, the Lord's Prayer, or those compiled in prayer books used in many church traditions. They aren't intended to be prefabricated messages or magical incantations, but rather maps that guide our minds to where they would never wander if left to themselves.

Some Christians think prayer is supposed to be spontaneous and using someone else's words is inauthentic. These same objections, however, are never applied to worship where we sing lyrics written by someone else. Is expressing ourselves to God using another's words allowed only when attached to a melody? And we should not forget that when Jesus' own disciples asked Him how to pray, our Lord taught them words to recite.

The Lord's Prayer is an excellent guide to focus our wandering minds, and perhaps the best place for any new Christian to begin their life of prayer. Jesus taught His followers to recite this prayer not because He didn't value authenticity or heartfelt prayers, but because He knew His followers needed more guidance. The Lord's Prayer is like the framing of a house. It provides the basic outline and structure for how to think about God and commune with Him. Without the Lord's Prayer, it's unlikely any of Jesus' Jewish followers would have thought to address God as "Our Father" which wasn't a common part of their Jewish prayer tradition. Likewise, I am unlikely to reflect on—let alone confess—sins of omission, were it not for this line from a daily prayer: "Most merciful God, we confess that we have sinned against you in thought, word, and deed, by what we have done, and by what we have left undone."[30]

The reason some Christian traditions don't affirm or utilize composed prayers is because they confuse spontaneity with authenticity. From the very earliest instructions about worship in the Old Testament, however, the Lord called His people to both heartfelt devotion and to structured praise. The structure provided by written prayers can guide us into deeper waters of communion with God.

 READ MORE Luke 11:1–4; 2 Samuel 7:18–29; Matthew 6:7–8

Consumer Christianity & Magical Prayer

Consumer God

Insert Prayers Here

32 IF JESUS WAS SERIOUS... THEN PRAYER IS NOT HOW WE CONTROL GOD.

THE USE OF PRE-WRITTEN prayers carries many benefits. They guide our often-wandering minds to focus on God. They instruct us to think rightly about our Lord with a depth we often lack. They can also remind us that communion with God is never to be a flippant, irreverent act, but one that embraces the paradox of His proximity and distance.

There is, however, one significant error that using written

prayers may unknowingly cause. Those with a highly transactional view of faith may view written prayers as incantations; magic spells that when spoken force God to act on one's behalf. Of course, the error is not with the prayers themselves but with the view of God carried by the person using them in this way.

God is not a divine vending machine in the sky that merely requires the exact change to dispense our desires, and prayer is not how we control God or win His favor. This is what differentiates Christian prayer from so many other religious rituals. Many religious practices approach God superstitiously. They assume God can be controlled if the right technique is employed or the proper words uttered. They see Him as a machine to be operated or a natural force to be harnessed, and therefore approach Him as a divine object. But we who belong to the living God approach Him as a divine person. He is our heavenly Father.

If your tendency has been to see prayer as a mechanical or magical form of divine control, then it may be best to avoid written prayers entirely or only utilize those that will dismantle the consumeristic view of God you may have inherited.

 READ MORE Matthew 6:5–8; Luke 18:1–8

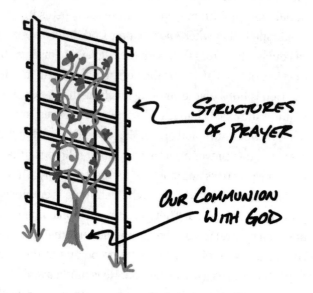

STRUCTURES OF PRAYER

OUR COMMUNION WITH GOD

33

IF JESUS WAS SERIOUS...
THEN A STRUCTURED PATTERN
OF PRAYER CAN CHANGE OUR
PERSPECTIVE.

IN ANCIENT ISRAEL, the normal practice was to set aside regular times for prayer in the morning, midday, and evening. Daniel used this prayer routine while a captive in Babylon, and it's what landed him in the lion's den (see Dan. 6). The tradition continued during the time of Jesus, and among the first generation of Jewish Christians. Later, the Jewish practice of praying at three intervals during the day became common throughout the church and was called "offices of prayer."

Eventually books of Christian prayers were compiled. The most popular among Protestants is *The Book of Common Prayer*, which includes readings from the Psalms, the Old Testament, the Epistles, and the Gospels for each day, along with prayers for morning, midday, and evening. The prayers and readings were organized around the seasons of the church calendar. This meant Christians dispersed throughout the world are nonetheless united in their reading of Scripture and prayers each day.

I have found numerous advantages in using a prayer book and observing the offices three times a day. First, it has been a helpful step toward Paul's command to "pray without ceasing" (1 Thess. 5:17). How often have the tasks of my day rushed at me like a pack of wild animals, and in a matter of seconds I am carried away by the stampede? By stopping at regular intervals during the day, pausing my work, and offering a few minutes to open the Bible and pray, I refocus my mind and soul toward God rather than toward less urgent matters of my day. It's a valuable way to gain perspective in our frenetic society.

Using the ancient offices of prayer and the church's calendar also reminds me that I cannot separate my union with God from my communion with His people. The writer of Hebrews speaks of the faithful who have preceded us as "a great cloud of witnesses" (Heb. 12:1) cheering us on from the stands.

Furthermore, using a tool like *The Book of Common Prayer* connects us to brothers and sisters who have prayed these same words for centuries before us. We are all one family—

one household of faith, with the same God and Father of all. Likewise, I also know that Christians throughout the world are praying and reflecting on the same words of Scripture each day. This thought lifts me from the individualism that haunts our culture and distorts many expressions of Christianity.

 READ MORE Hebrews 12:1–2; Daniel 6:10–13

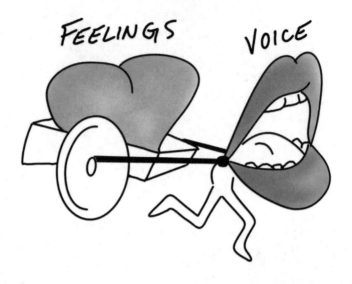

FEELINGS   VOICE

34 IF JESUS WAS SERIOUS...
THEN SINGING IS ALSO A FORM
OF PRAYER.

IN ACTS 16, PAUL AND SILAS were stripped and beaten
with rods many times for proclaiming Jesus in the city of Philippi.
Then they were thrown in jail and their feet put in stocks. I can
only imagine the misery of their circumstances—naked, beaten,
chained, and imprisoned. That's what makes their response so
odd. "About midnight Paul and Silas were praying and singing
hymns to God" (Acts 16:25).

I would understand if they were moaning and complaining

to God, or even crying out and pleading with God. But singing? That strikes modern readers as strange because we associate singing with positivity, joyfulness, and celebration. What was there to celebrate about being beaten and incarcerated?

We usually think of singing and praying as two distinct acts. Prayer is what we do when we need something from God, and singing is what we do when He grants it. We've been taught to associate prayer with petition and singing with praise. This clear distinction, however, is a recent development. Limiting singing to joyful expressions is a trait of consumeristic religion that peddles in positivity, but the Bible has a far larger vision of why we sing.

In Jesus' ancient Jewish culture, singing was a means of lament and even complaint, not merely praise. Just read the book of Psalms—which was the prayer book used by ancient Jews, including Jesus and His first followers. The Psalms are a collection of prayers that were sung to God. Some were joyful, but more were expressions of misery, confession, doubt, or grief. So we should not understand Silas and Paul "praying and singing" in prison as two separate acts of petition and praise. Instead, these are two expressions of the same desire—to connect with God amid their suffering. In other words, singing was itself an act of prayer.

The scene in Acts 16 reminds us that sometimes singing, like prayer, is a discipline. We don't always sing in response to God's action, but in anticipation of it. Henri Nouwen said a discipline is "the effort to create some space in which God can act."[31] In their misery at midnight in the Philippian jail, Paul and Silas needed hope and they longed for God's intervention.

They sang to shift their focus from their pain to God's presence, and to create space for Him to act within them.

We all face midnights of the soul when our circumstances are dark, when our hearts become cold toward God, when we do not feel like singing, and when we cannot form the words to pray. That is precisely when we ought to sing and allow the words of a songwriter or a psalmist to guide our hearts toward communion with God. In the darkness we begin with our voices and allow our hearts to follow.

READ MORE **Acts 16:19–25; Psalm 42:5–8**

IF JESUS WAS SERIOUS...
35 **THEN PRAYER WILL HELP US NOTICE GOD EVERYWHERE WE GO.**

IN 1999, TWO COGNITIVE psychologists conducted an experiment now widely called the "invisible gorilla" test. People watching a video of a basketball team were asked to count the number of times the ball was passed between the players. Partway through the video, a person in a gorilla suit walked through the team thumping its chest as players passed the ball. About half of those watching the video were so focused on counting passes they never noticed the gorilla. The study concluded that our minds are wired to see what we *expect* to see and often miss what we do not *intend* to encounter.[32]

Prayer trains us to see God where we might otherwise miss Him. Without it, in our busy, information-overloaded culture, it is very easy to focus on everything *other than* God. We can be so focused on the news, our work, or the 10,000 things vying for our attention that we may go days and even weeks without seeing God in our lives. Of course, that doesn't mean He isn't there. Like the gorilla, He might be in the middle of our busy life thumping His chest to get our attention, but we never take our eye off the ball long enough to see Him. Prayer is a time to slow down, refocus, and notice God's presence.

There are certain forms of prayer that can train us to recognize God in the ordinary routines of our day. For example, one tradition invites Christians to reflect on the events, encounters, and feelings that filled their day. With intention we replay the previous hours and ask ourselves questions to uncover the hidden movements of God that might otherwise have gone unnoticed. The practice is often done at the end of the day, although some like to start each morning with the discipline in anticipation of the events ahead.

A simple way to begin is by reviewing your calendar to bring to mind the events and activities of your completed day. As you reflect, ask God's Spirit to reveal how He was present in each task or encounter. When were you aware of His presence, and when were you not? How might a particular activity have been different if you'd been aware of God being with you? Over time this practice of reflection and daily examination will help you be more aware of God's presence *during* the day and not simply at the close of it.

 READ MORE Genesis 28:10–16; Mark 8:14–21

Spiritual Narcissism   *"Search Me, O Lord"*

36 IF JESUS WAS SERIOUS...
THEN PRAYER IS ALSO A DISCIPLINE
OF SELF-AWARENESS.

WE HAVE BEEN EXPLORING the important role prayer has
in making us aware of God and His presence with us, but prayer
is also a critical way we become more aware of ourselves. Both
are necessary for real communion with God. In prayer we
bring our true self into the presence of the true God. One form
of prayer that helps us do this is called the *Prayer of Examen*.
It's an odd word that most will associate with *examination*,

which brings to mind unpleasant memories from school or the doctor's office.

Examen comes from the Latin word for the indicator on a balance scale. It means to reveal the truth. The Prayer of Examen, when properly understood, is intended to reveal the truth within us. It is not a test—at least not in the pass/ fail sense. Instead, it is the uncovering of hidden or forgotten things so that we may engage God truthfully.

Like all Christian prayer, the Examen is not an activity we undertake alone. It is not mere self-examination or self-awareness, which is fashionable in these times of spiritual narcissism. The Prayer of Examen means welcoming God into every part of our lives so that He may do His revealing work in us and with us, and it is something Scripture speaks about repeatedly.

David told his son to serve the Lord faithfully because "the LORD searches all hearts and understands every plan and thought" (1 Chron. 28:9). And David famously prayed, "O LORD, you have searched me and known me!" (Ps. 139:1). The king went on in the same prayer to invite God to "try me" (Ps. 139:23). He asks the Lord to examine his heart, his thoughts, and to expose any evil so that he might be led in the right direction. David models for us the Prayer of Examen and shows how it is done in cooperation with the Lord, who alone can see and reveal all things.

I encourage you to reflect on David's words in Psalm 139. Invite God's Spirit to search you and reveal things—both good and sinful—that you may have hidden or ignored.

 READ MORE   Psalm 139:1–24; 1 Chronicles 28:9

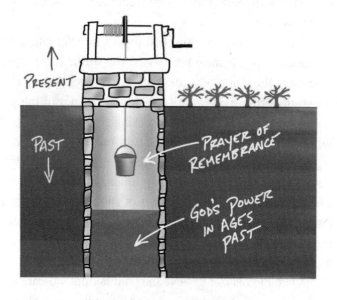

PRESENT

PAST

PRAYER OF REMEMBRANCE

GOD'S POWER IN AGES PAST

37 IF JESUS WAS SERIOUS... THEN REMEMBERING IS MORE THAN A MENTAL EXERCISE.

ONE OF THE MOST repeated commandments of the Bible is to remember. In the Old Testament, the Israelites were told to remember God's deliverance from slavery through the celebration of the Passover. They were commanded to remember His Law by meditating on it day and night. And after they had crossed the Jordan River into the promised land, the Lord told them to erect stones of remembrance so future generations would remember His faithfulness.

The Hebrew understanding of remembrance, however, was very different from our own. It was far more than a cognitive exercise or recollection. Paul Bradshaw, a theologian, puts it this way: "In the Jewish world, remembrance was not a purely mental activity . . . it was not simply about nostalgia for the past . . . but about asking God to remember His people and complete His saving purpose today."[33] To remember meant to bring all the power from the past event into the present.

This Hebraic understanding of remembrance should change the way we read Jesus' words to His disciples at the Last Supper. After explaining that the bread and wine represented His broken body and shed blood for the forgiveness of sin, Jesus said, "Do this in remembrance of me" (Luke 22:19). The communion table is supposed to be more than an act of mental recollection of the cross. Scripture is clear that Jesus "died . . . once for all" (Rom. 6:10) and remembering His death through the table does not repeat His sacrifice, but it does bring the power of His sacrifice into the present.

You might be wondering: What does this have to do with prayer? While it is important to recall how God has acted on behalf of His people in the past through the Exodus, the giving of the Law, and the cross, we should also recall God's past faithfulness in our own lives and that of our community. The Prayer of Examen is the practice of remembering God's presence and actions in the past—the past day, the past week, the past year.

This prayer of remembrance, while certainly provoking our gratitude and praise, is also a means of inviting God's presence and saving power into today. It is a way of saying, "Lord, in the past You have been faithful and good. Help me to see Your faithfulness and goodness again. Be the same God You were yesterday, today."

 READ MORE **Luke 22:14–19; Joshua 4:1–7**

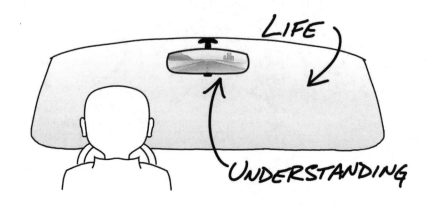

38 IF JESUS WAS SERIOUS...
THEN REFLECTING ON THE PAST
BUILDS FAITH FOR THE FUTURE.

AS JESUS WASHED the disciples' feet, He came to Peter who resisted the act of humble service. Jesus said to him, "What I am doing you do not understand now, but afterward you will understand" (John 13:7). I wonder if Jesus was only referring to the foot washing, or perhaps the entirety of Peter's time with Jesus. Peter was, after all, a slow learner and often misinterpreted Jesus' words and actions—sometimes spectacularly.

Jesus' words to Peter remind me of what Søren Kierkegaard

said: "Life can only be understood backwards; but it must be lived forwards."[34] This fact poses a problem for those of us who prefer to understand everything before we act. It also does not bode well for those who do not take the time to reflect on the past and learn from their experiences.

The Prayer of Examen is a discipline to help us understand backwards. It is often practiced at night before sleep by recollecting the events of the day—activities, conversations, encounters, and emotions. As we replay these events in our mind, we also invite the Holy Spirit to reveal things we may not have noticed at the time. As we look back on the day through the illumination of the Spirit, we may come to new understandings of the people and circumstances we encountered. This will almost always prompt new prayers of gratitude, intercession, confession, or serenity.

I may confess indifference toward the man who served me lunch. I may sense pain in a colleague's conversation at work and pray for her. I may realize God was especially near as I watered the plants in the late evening and thank Him for that quiet moment of illumination. I may acknowledge that my busy tasks were a way to distract myself from some lingering sadness.

Wisdom is granted to us from God's Spirit as we gain understanding from looking backwards. Try this practice tonight, and if you need help, consider using your calendar as you pray over each event and encounter. You may have lived your day forward, but you may come to understand it very differently by praying through it backwards.

 READ MORE John 13:1–5; Romans 8:31–39

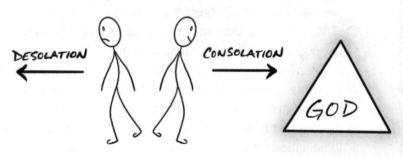

PRAYER OF EXAMEN

DESOLATION ← CONSOLATION →

GOD

TODAY — WHEN DID I FEEL BEING DRAWN NEAR TO GOD?
— WHEN DID I FEEL BEING DRAWN AWAY FROM GOD?

39 IF JESUS WAS SERIOUS... THEN PRAYER CAN REVEAL WHAT DRAWS US TOWARD GOD OR AWAY FROM HIM.

AS YOU EXAMINE your day, one filter involves looking for moments of what Ignatius Loyola called *consolation*. He defined those as times when you are moving toward God. Inversely, he called moments of movement away from God *desolation*. During a time of Examen, the goal is to identify what activities or moments drew you closer to God or sparked an awareness of

His presence, and what activities regularly distracted you from any sense of God. Being more aware of both of these movements can help you live with greater intentionality and aid you in developing a continual communion with Him.

I have found it helpful to use a series of questions to uncover the deeper feelings I've accumulated during the day, as well as the movements of consolation or desolation I've experienced. For example, as you play back the events of the day like a video in your mind ask yourself, Where was I most *alive* today? Or *loved*, *sad*, *grateful*, or *anxious*? Allow these questions to prompt prayers of thanksgiving, confession, or petition.

A struggle many people have with this practice is honesty. Very often we will think back to a conversation or event from the day and dwell upon how we *should* have acted or what we *ought* to have said. The goal of Examen is not to reflect on what could, should, or ought to have happened, but rather to be honest with oneself, with the Holy Spirit's help, about what *did* happen and how you actually felt.

Here are a few suggested questions to begin your prayers of Examen and remembrance:

Desolation—the sense of God's absence

When, today, did I sense being drawn away from God?

When did I feel most dissatisfied and restricted today?

Was there any time today when I felt discouraged?

What was the most draining part of my day?

Was there time today when I felt guilty, ashamed, or lonely?

Consolation—the sense of God's presence

When, today, did I feel closest to the presence of God?

What events, relationships, or thoughts of the day drew me nearer to God?

When did I feel most free?

What was the most life-giving part of my day?

What was most joyful about my day?

 READ MORE 2 Corinthians 13:5–10; Galatians 6:1–5

PART 5

THE TRUTH (& NOTHING BUT THE TRUTH) SO HELP ME GOD

He also told this parable to some who trusted in themselves that they were righteous, and treated others with contempt:

"Two men went up into the temple to pray, one a Pharisee and the other a tax collector. The Pharisee, standing by himself, prayed thus: 'God, I thank you that I am not like other men, extortioners, unjust, adulterers, or even like this tax collector. I fast twice a week; I give tithes of all that I get.' But the tax collector, standing far off, would not even lift up his eyes to heaven, but beat his breast, saying, 'God, be merciful to me, a sinner!' I tell you, this man went down to his house justified, rather than the other. For everyone who exalts himself will be humbled, but the one who humbles himself will be exalted."

IF JESUS WAS SERIOUS...

40 IF JESUS WAS SERIOUS... THEN CONFESSION IS HOW WE SHATTER OUR ILLUSIONS ABOUT OURSELVES.

SOME CHRISTIANS, especially from traditions that focus on a "personal relationship" with God, have a difficult time with confession. They often emphasize the atoning death of Jesus on the cross and the sufficiency of His blood to cover their sins, and therefore fear the practice of confession might diminish the cross in some way. I've often heard Christians dismiss confession because, "God has already forgiven all of my sins—past, present, and future—on the cross." Some even view confession as an attempt to earn God's forgiveness through human work, and therefore a diminishment of His grace. Others have abandoned the practice as illogical: "If God already knows everything, why do I have to tell Him my sins?"

All of these excuses suffer from two errors. First, they ignore the fact that Scripture plainly commands us to confess our sins both to God and each other. And, second, they fundamentally misunderstand the purpose of confession.

Prayers of confession are not magical incantations that somehow control God or force His mercy to flow. Neither does our admission of sin diminish His grace in any way, nor do our prayers add to the redemption accomplished by Jesus on the cross. And, obviously, our prayers never add to God's knowledge, which is already complete.

To *confess* means "to say the same thing." When we confess our sins we are merely admitting what God already knows to be true about us. Therefore, the practice is not commanded for His benefit but for *ours*. In this way, confession is a lot like the discipline of generosity. We are commanded to give not because God needs our gifts—the earth is the Lord's and everything in it—but because generosity transforms the heart of the one who gives.

Likewise, confession is a vital means of growing us into God's likeness by first seeing and then admitting what is *unlike* God in our lives. It is a discipline that forces us to abandon the false self-image we'd prefer to believe so that we must gaze at our true self. The human capacity for self-deception is almost limitless, and if left unchecked it can transplant us into a fantasy in which we need no grace and where we are always righteous, always correct, and always pure.

Confession shatters this fantasy with sober self-assessment guided by our sisters and brothers and the Holy Spirit. Together, we are gently led to first see and then speak the truth about ourselves. As we do, God's grace meets us. This grace reminds us that we are loved as we are, sin and all, even as it spurs us forward toward what we are called to become.

 READ MORE James 5:13–16; Psalm 51:1–19

PRAYER MASKS

THE FERVENT FAKER

THE PIOUS PRETENDER

THE HAPPY HYPOCRITE

WHAT IS REALLY IN ME

GOD

WHAT GOD SEES BUT WE FEAR TO ADMIT

**41 IF JESUS WAS SERIOUS...
THEN WE CANNOT
HIDE OUR TRUE SELF FROM GOD.**

MANY OF THE BEST-KNOWN and celebrated characters in the Bible were scoundrels. King David, for example, possessed some noble qualities, but he was also a liar, adulterer, and murderer. Still, he was called "a man after God's own heart" (1 Sam. 13:14). The explanation may be found in David's prayers. They run the spectrum from adoration to anger, and from contrition to contempt. In other words, David's prayers were profoundly human and uncomfortably honest. He expressed the truth about himself to God—the good, the bad, and the ugly.

The courage to abandon the pretense and reveal ourselves truthfully to God is a mark of mature faith. However, many of us still approach God in prayer the way we approach church on Sunday. We make ourselves presentable, we clean up our children and our language, and we pretend to be someone we are not. Of course, it's silly to masquerade before an all-knowing, all-seeing God. So why do we?

When we feel the need to manufacture a facade of piety in our prayers, it isn't because we are afraid God will not accept us but because *we* cannot accept ourselves. We want to maintain the imaginary self we have created rather than face our true self with its failures, shortcomings, and sins. The imaginary self can be very successful in the world, and may even be celebrated by the church, but it can never truly pray because our Lord only welcomes the company of real sinners and never imaginary saints.

C. S. Lewis said, "We must lay before Him what is in us, not what ought to be in us."[35] This is what David modeled in his prayers. So, what is in you today?

 READ MORE **Psalm 32:1–5; John 4:23–24**

42 IF JESUS WAS SERIOUS...
THEN HIDING OUR SIN WILL
DISRUPT OUR PRAYERS MORE THAN
THE SIN ITSELF WILL.

"THE YOUNGER GENERATION has had it with fakery."[36]
That's how Mary DeMuth responded when asked about
the recent flood of church leadership scandals in the news.
Unlike previous generations that also experienced abusive
or duplicitous clergy but chose to remain connected to the

church, more young people are abandoning the institutional church altogether.

DeMuth's observation applies well beyond church scandals. There is a rising desire for authenticity and transparency in our culture even as public trust in leaders and institutions continues to decline, and as social media conditions more of us to present fake portraits of our daily lives. Ironically, we crave authenticity at precisely the moment when our corrupt institutions and superficial social media are the least prepared to supply it.

In this environment, the authenticity of the Bible can be both refreshing and uncomfortable. Many prayers in Scripture are outbursts of anger toward God over injustices, abuses, and the perception that He has acted unfairly. For example, after accepting the Lord's call to be a prophet, Jeremiah faced rejection from the people. His anger toward God was palpable: "O LORD, you have deceived me, and I was deceived; you are stronger than I, and you have prevailed. I have become a laughingstock all the day; everyone mocks me" (Jer. 20:7).

Have you ever prayed like that? Have you ever shaken your fist at God, called Him names, or accused Him of malice? If so, you're in good company with many biblical heroes and about a quarter of the Psalms. Prayer means admitting and offering to God what is really in us—no matter how ugly it might be.

The world is where many of us pretend. Prayer is where we ought to be real. There is no point masking your anger, fear, or sin from God. He sees it anyway. This is why Richard Foster advises us to pray to God even when soaked in ungodliness.

"We lift even our disobedience into the arms of the Father; he is strong enough to carry the weight. Sin, to be sure, separates us from God, but trying to hide our sin separates us all the more."[37]

 READ MORE **Jeremiah 20:7–18; Psalm 88:1–18**

IMMATURE
CONFESSION

PIT OF
SIN

ESCAPE CONSEQUENCES

MATURE
CONFESSION

REUNION WITH GOD

43 IF JESUS WAS SERIOUS...
THEN THE GOAL OF CONFESSION
IS RECONCILIATION, NOT JUST
ATONEMENT.

WALTER ARRIVED AT MY CHURCH office without an appointment. He was not a member of our church and had never attended a Sunday service, but he eagerly wanted "to meet with a pastor." He opened up surprisingly quickly with two confessions. First, he wasn't "really into religion." Second, Walter admitted to an inappropriate relationship with one of his employees. This caused a lot of problems for his business, which was now losing money, and his business partner, a Christian, was angry when he discovered Walter's transgression.

He told Walter that in order to make things right, and for God to bless their business again, he should make a large donation to a church. So, as he sat in my office, Walter pulled out his checkbook and asked me, "How much should I give to the church?"

Walter's instincts are not uncommon and they reveal a popular misunderstanding about confession. While he wanted to make an atonement for his sin, Walter's goal was *not* reconciliation with God. Ultimately, he simply wanted his business to thrive, and his partner had convinced him that an offering for his sin would appease God's anger and restore His blessing. (In case you're wondering, I did not accept his check.)

Here's the point—there is a difference between confessing sin, atoning for sin, and reconciliation with God. Many of us feel guilty about our transgressions, and many of us would like to escape the consequences of our sinful decisions. That may lead us to confess in prayer to God or in person to a spiritual mentor. Far fewer of us, however, actually want our sins removed so that we might live again in communion with God.

That's what made David's prayer of confession in Psalm 51 so remarkable. Like Walter, he wanted his sin removed, but David desired its removal for a very different reason. He wasn't merely interested in avoiding the unpleasant consequences of his behavior. David confessed so that he might be reconciled to God. He was called, "A man after God's own heart" not because he did not sin, but because David longed for the Lord Himself, and not merely the Lord's blessings.

The writer of Hebrews says that we ought to be "looking to Jesus" (Heb. 12:2). He is to be the goal we strive after, like a runner runs a race. And, therefore, we ought to avoid sin which acts like thorny vines tangled around our legs preventing us from reaching Him. Confession is one of the ways we cut those vines, but the *reason* we cut them is to draw nearer to God.

 READ MORE **Psalm 51:1–19; Hebrews 12:1–2**

WHAT I OFFER IN PRAYER TO GOD

WHAT'S REALLY IN ME

44 **IF JESUS WAS SERIOUS...
THEN WE MUST BE ATTENTIVE TO
OUR INNER CESSPOOL.**

SCRIPTURE IS FULL OF PEOPLE confessing their sins—
both individually and corporately. It is modeled in both the Old
and New Testaments, and the apostles write multiple times that
we are to confess our sins. Confession is supposed to be a regular, habitual pattern in our life with God. Why then is it so rarely
practiced?

Some church traditions utilize a liturgy in worship that
includes reciting a prayer of confession. This has real benefit,

but it can also become an empty practice if divorced from a genuine awareness of our sins and heartfelt repentance. In most churches I've attended, confession in any form was non-existent. At best it was something only referred to in the past tense. "As a younger man I _____, but God rescued me from that sin years ago." Speaking of our sin in the present tense is frowned upon unless stripped of all specificity and rendered utterly inoffensive.

And yet, if we are to develop a praying life of genuine communion with God we must present our true selves to Him. We must admit what is actually within us—including the sinful, evil, and grotesque. We must develop a habit of confession. Doing this, however, means welcoming the discomfort of self-examination.

Years ago a friend shared with me a vivid dream. "I was walking along the seashore," he told me, "when I reached into the water and pulled up a large, ugly rock covered in seaweed and barnacles. I carefully removed them and washed the rock in the surf revealing a beautiful stone." My friend believed the dream was a metaphor representing his life. He'd recently committed to following Jesus, and he'd worked hard to remove the obvious sin in this life.

"I knew that stone was me," he said. "I was proud of how I'd changed and that I'd become a better man." But that wasn't the end of the dream. "Jesus was with me on the beach," he continued. "I handed Him the stone. Rather than being impressed with its beauty, he cracked the stone on his knee and opened it and showed me the inside. It was full of ugly, rotten things."

The message was clear, and it's one we find in the Gospels: Jesus isn't interested in people who merely appear clean on the outside. He wants to clean us from the inside. Part of that process is admitting the ugly things that abide within us and confessing them to our Lord in prayer. As C. S. Lewis said, "The true Christian's nostril is to be continually attentive to the inner cesspool."[38]

 READ MORE Matthew 23:25–28; 1 John 1:5–10

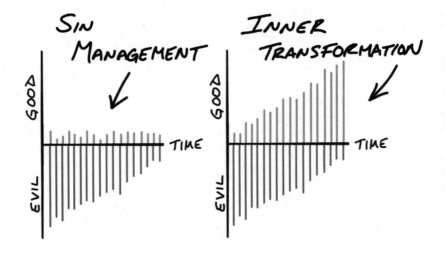

IF JESUS WAS SERIOUS...

45 THEN SIN IS ALSO THE GOOD WE FAIL TO DO.

THE BOOK OF COMMON PRAYER includes a prayer of confession that has been used by Christians for centuries, and which I have found incredibly helpful in my communion with God. It begins:

> Most merciful God,
> we confess that we have sinned against you
> in thought, word, and deed,
> by what we have done,
> and by what we have left undone.

When reflected upon, this single sentence can push us to consider the depths of our sin well beyond the one-dimensional view we've inherited from the shallow doctrinal puddles of consumer Christianity. For example, here we are reminded that sin isn't limited to our behaviors. It may also infect our thoughts and words. As Jesus taught, it isn't enough to not murder (an action); we are also called to not cultivate anger in our hearts (an attitude).

Similarly, the prayer acknowledges that we sin not only with our actions but also our failure to take action. This idea was concisely captured by the anonymous pundit who said, "The only thing necessary for the triumph of evil is for good men to do nothing."[39] It is self-evident that evil is evil, but Burke was acknowledging that passivity in the face of evil is also evil.

Historically, Christians have affirmed this fact by recognizing both sins of commission (things we do, but shouldn't), and sins of omission (things we don't do, but should). A shallow faith simply seeks to avoid bad behavior, but a mature faith seeks to cultivate what is good, true, and beautiful in the world. Failure to do these positive actions is not merely missing an opportunity to manifest God's kingdom on earth; it is also sin.

As you examine yourself in prayer today, ask the Spirit to reveal how you have failed to live in accordance with your calling in Christ through both your action and your inaction.

 READ MORE **James 4:17; 1 John 3:17–18**

46 IF JESUS WAS SERIOUS... THEN WE WILL OWN OUR SINS AND THOSE OF OUR COMMUNITY.

DANIEL IS ONE OF THE more fascinating figures in the Bible. Virtually every other leading character in the Old Testament failed in some dramatic way. This was true of Abraham, Moses, Noah, and David. Each one, no matter how deep their faith, is depicted as disobeying God at some point. But not Daniel. That's not to say he never sinned, but the writers of the Old Testament depict him—from childhood to old age—as perhaps the most loyal, faithful, and righteous man in the Bible—apart from Jesus, of course.

That's what makes his prayer of confession in Daniel 9 so remarkable. God's people were guilty of many terrible sins including idolatry, abandoning God's commands, and turning away from their covenant with Him. We have no evidence, however, that Daniel ever participated in any of these rebellious acts. That's what makes his prayer of confession so unusual. When Daniel confesses the many sins of the people *he includes himself in their wickedness*. He begins: "*We* have sinned and done wrong and acted wickedly and rebelled, turning aside from your commandments and rules" (Dan. 9:5, emphasis added). His pronouns throughout the prayer are *we*, *our*, and *us*. He never uses the words *they* or *their*. Why does he include himself in the sins of the people if he never committed them?

This is particularly difficult for individualistic Americans to grasp, but Daniel never understood his relationship with God to be only private or personal. God called *a people* to himself—a community. Therefore, Daniel saw his connection with God as fundamentally corporate. To be united with God meant being united with God's people as well. In the same way, Jesus came not only to share in our humanity, but also to carry our depravity. Like Daniel, he was innocent but accepted the burden for sins that were not his own. Scripture teaches us this uncomfortable truth: we cannot claim the blessings of our community but deny the burden of its sins.

For example, I live in the United States. Most Americans are eager to accept the benefits of this land even though we are probably not personally responsible for any of them, but we are reluctant to own the sins of America because we did not directly participate in them. I am quick to point my finger at the horrors of slavery, greed, racism, injustice, genocide, and dehumanization because I did not commit those evils. Yet these sins are mingled with America's virtues, and I am certainly the indirect beneficiary of both.

Confession, at least in its biblical form, cannot be an individual exercise even when practiced alone. It must always be done with our community in mind.

 READ MORE **Daniel 9:1–6; 1 Peter 2:9–10**

PART 6

PRAYER CHANGES (HOW YOU SEE) THE WORLD

And they went to a place called Gethsemane. And he said to his disciples, "Sit here while I pray."

And he took with him Peter and James and John, and began to be greatly distressed and troubled. And he said to them, "My soul is very sorrowful, even to death. Remain here and watch." And going a little farther, he fell on the ground and prayed that, if it were possible, the hour might pass from him.

And he said, "Abba, Father, all things are possible for you. Remove this cup from me. Yet not what I will, but what you will."

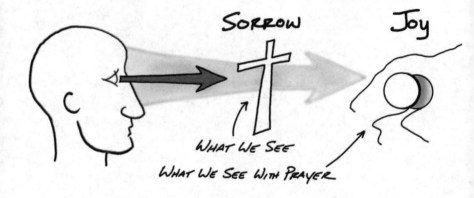

SORROW

Joy

WHAT WE SEE

WHAT WE SEE WITH PRAYER

47 IF JESUS WAS SERIOUS...
THEN PRAYER WILL HELP US SEE
PAST OUR PAIN.

ON THE NIGHT Jesus was betrayed, but before the soldiers
came to arrest Him, He prayed in anguish to His Father in a
garden of olive trees. He was very aware of what was ahead—
humiliation, abandonment, torture, and death. The gravity of the
moment was reflected in the brutal honesty of His prayer: "Abba,
Father, all things are possible for you. Remove this cup from me"
(Mark 14:36). Jesus did not want to suffer. He did not want to die.
This was Jesus at His most human, His most vulnerable.

The scene echoes one from much earlier in the Bible. In another garden, another man faced a similar decision between following God's will or His own. Rather than surrendering himself to the love of God, Adam, like every person since, rejected the will of God to declare, "*My* will be done!" His disobedience, which represents our own, unleashed sin, evil, and death into creation.

Jesus, whom Scripture calls the second Adam, inverted the first Adam's rebellion. While honestly confessing His desire to not follow His Father's plan to the cross, Jesus nonetheless surrendered Himself to God. He chose to abandon His preference and ventured everything on the goodness, love, and power of His heavenly Father. "Not my will, but *yours* be done."

The agony Jesus expressed in the garden fulfilled what Isaiah had prophesied about the Messiah centuries earlier. "He was despised and rejected by men, a man of sorrows and acquainted with grief" (Isa. 53:3). But this picture of Jesus in Gethsemane is incomplete. It captures only part of what Jesus saw that night amid the olive trees.

According to the author of Hebrews, intermingled with Jesus' sorrow over His looming death, there was also a vision of the victory beyond. Scripture says that Jesus accepted the cross and its shame, "for the joy that was set before him" (Heb. 12:2). Somehow, in communion with the Father that night, Jesus was able to face the agony of His execution because He could see what was on the other side of the cross. He saw the empty tomb. He saw His ascension to the Father. He saw Himself enthroned over creation with all power and authority. And He saw every knee in heaven and earth bowing and every tongue confessing that He was King (Phil. 2:10–11).

In the garden we find a central paradox of the Christian faith—that by surrendering Himself to the darkness of the world Jesus overcame it. And like Him, sometimes we may cry out to God in prayer to "remove this cup from me," but rather than changing our circumstances sometimes He gives us eyes to see beyond them. Through prayer He shows us the coming dawn that will overwhelm our present darkness. And this joy that is set before us is all we need to rise and take the next step forward.

 READ MORE Hebrews 12:1–2; Philippians 2:5–11

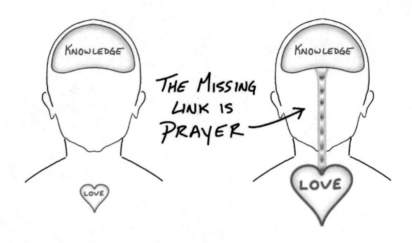

48 IF JESUS WAS SERIOUS...
THEN KNOWLEDGE ALONE WILL
NOT TRANSFORM US.

DURING MY JUNIOR YEAR of college I had a crisis of faith—
or maybe it should be called a crisis of facts. For years I had been
studying the history, theology, and doctrines of Christianity. I
was excelling past many of my peers in Bible knowledge, and
this was all while simultaneously studying Islam, Buddhism,
Judaism, and humanist philosophy as a Comparative Religion
major at a state university.

I believed that filling my mind with Christian knowledge

would automatically translate into Christian virtue. After all, that is what most churches and ministries are designed to do. We send our kids to "Sunday School," we sit passively in worship services and listen to an expert "teach" Scripture for forty minutes, and we attend "Bible Studies." All of this knowledge was supposed to transform me into a righteous person. But it didn't.

By my 21st year, I recognized little change in my own feelings or behaviors. How was Jesus able to overcome His fears of death in the garden, and after years of studying Scripture I still couldn't overcome my social fear of acceptance in college? Adding to my growing disillusionment with facts was my septuagenarian professor of New Testament whose biblical knowledge far exceeded my own, and yet he remained definitively *un*christian in his attitudes and actions. Knowledge alone, I was discovering, wasn't enough. I'm not saying knowledge isn't significant. I'm saying it isn't *sufficient*. The model of the Christian life I'd been given was incomplete.

As this truth became apparent to me, I slipped into a season of deep reflection and searching. I became less enthusiastic about the student ministry I'd been a leader within, because it didn't seem equipped to address the widening gap between my knowledge and my character. It was teaching me *about* Jesus, but was incapable of making me *like* Jesus. I was experiencing the profound truth of the old Sioux proverb: "The longest journey you will make in your life is from your head to your heart."

It was in this season, as I reflected back on my experiences in churches and ministries, that it occurred to me no one ever taught me how to pray. I had been shown how to study the Bible, how to debate nonbelievers, and how to defend my faith, but I'd never been shown what communion with God actually looks like. *Maybe prayer was the missing piece*, I thought. *Maybe prayer was the conduit through which knowledge could pass from my head into my heart.* This question began a new phase in my life with Christ, and it opened me to a far larger vision of faith.

It was as if I'd spent the preceding years in the foyer of a house believing there was nothing more. My tradition had welcomed me into God's home, but had never shown me the splendid rooms beyond the front door. I'd been sleeping on the foyer floor, unaware of the bedrooms upstairs. I'd been cooking meals on a fire with kindling on the tile, not knowing a full kitchen was steps away. Prayer opened new doors and illuminated new rooms.

If you have been struggling and hungry for a deeper faith, a life *with* God not merely a life full of knowledge *about* Him, you must pray. Prayer is the conduit between our head and our heart. It is the catalyst that changes mere knowledge into love, and love into action.

 READ MORE **Luke 11:1–13; 1 Corinthians 8:1–3**

49 IF JESUS WAS SERIOUS...
THEN PRAYER WILL CHANGE US,
NOT JUST OUR CIRCUMSTANCES.

PAUL AND SILAS HAD BEEN arrested, beaten, and thrown
into prison with their feet chained. Throughout the night, not
knowing what fate awaited them in the morning, the apostles
"were praying and singing hymns to God." Then a miracle
occurred. An earthquake shook the prison, the doors flew
open, and their chains fell off. When the jailer awoke and saw
the prison doors open, he assumed Paul and Silas had escaped.
Knowing death awaited him for failing in his duty, the jailer drew

his sword to kill himself. But from the darkness Paul yelled, "Do not harm yourself, for we are all here." The jailer then fell down before them and said, "Sirs, what must I do to be saved?" (Acts 16:25–30).

When reading this story from Acts 16, most assume the miracle was the earthquake that opened the doors and broke Paul's and Silas's chains, but that isn't the case. The true miracle was that Paul and Silas *chose not to escape* when given the chance. It wasn't the earthquake that led to the jailer's conversion. He thought the earthquake was just bad luck. Instead, it was the disciples' decision to *stay in the dungeon* that confused and stunned the jailer.

He must have wondered, *What kind of men would willingly choose a prison cell when the door to freedom literally opened before them? And what kind of men show concern for the well-being of their captor?* Paul and Silas clearly possessed a power and a love the jailor had never encountered before. That is what led him to fall on his knees and transfer his allegiance from Caesar to Jesus.

We often pray because we want God to change our circumstances. We want Him to shake our world, open doors, and break our chains. God's purpose in prayer, however, may be different. Rather than changing our circumstances, prayer just as often changes our *vision* of our circumstances. In communion with Christ, we may begin to see things from a different, more divine, perspective. A challenge begins to look more like an opportunity. Our enemy is transformed into our neighbor. That great fear becomes a catalyst for greater faith. A dark prison cell becomes a sanctuary where we experience God's presence.

I suspect that is why Paul and Silas didn't run when the doors opened and their chains fell off. They weren't praying in their cell because they wanted to be released. They were praying to draw closer to Christ, and He was already powerfully present with them in the jail cell. They knew, whether prisoners or paroled, whether slaves or free, they belonged to Christ and He would never abandon them. And through prayer, they came to see the jailor not as their enemy, but as a man like any other in need of mercy and God's love.

What circumstances are you asking God to change? Invite Him to change your vision of those circumstances instead.

READ MORE **Acts 16:25–34; Philippians 4:10–13**

"IF WE'RE NOT ABLE TO BE ALONE, WE'RE GOING TO BE MORE LONELY." — SHERRY TURKLE

PERSON A: ALWAYS LONELY

[ ]

PERSON B: NOT LONELY

[| | | | | | | | | | | | |]

☐ SOCIAL   ☐ SOLITUDE

50 IF JESUS WAS SERIOUS... THEN BEING ALONE WILL TRANSFORM OUR LONELINESS.

JESUS PRAYED ALONE while in the garden of Gethsemane, but He wasn't entirely alone. He brought Peter, James, and John with Him to keep watch as He prayed. We see this pattern throughout the Gospels. Jesus often went to a solitary place to pray, but then emerged to engage His followers and to minister to the crowds. His habit was to move from solitude to community and back again.

Recent surveys have uncovered what researchers are calling

a "loneliness epidemic" in wealthy societies. More people than ever are reporting a chronic feeling of isolation, and the solution would appear simple—just be more social. The data, however, reveals a far more interesting and counterintuitive response to loneliness. One survey in the U.S., for example, found those over age 65 are the most likely to live alone, but they are also the least likely to report feeling lonely. In contrast, young people between 18 and 22—traditionally the most social as well as the most prolific users of social media—are the most likely to report "often or always" feeling alone.[40] It seems constant engagement with others isn't the antidote to loneliness.

A few years ago I heard Sherry Turkle speak on the subject at a conference. Turkle is a professor of the Social Studies of Science and Technology at MIT and a clinical psychologist. She has spent years researching the impact of technology on people and relationships. When the internet and social media first emerged, Turkle was an outspoken advocate believing these tools would bring people together, overcome social barriers, and build empathy. Her research, however, showed precisely the opposite.

The problem with smartphones that keep us connected to everything and everywhere, says Turkle, is that they eliminate boredom. Moments of silent boredom are when we face what's really inside of us—our fears, joys, beliefs, and struggles. In other words, boredom is necessary for self-awareness. This self-awareness, Turkle argues, then equips us to have intimate connections with others. Only when I know who I am can I share the deepest parts of myself with another. The constant stimulation of mobile tech is interrupting this process.

Turkle says we must "cultivate the capacity for solitude, the ability to be separate, to gather yourself. Solitude is where you find yourself so that you can reach out to other people and form real attachments. When we don't have the capacity for solitude, we turn to other people in order to feel less anxious or in order to feel alive. When this happens, we're not able to appreciate who they are. It's as though we're using them as spare parts to support our fragile sense of self. We slip into thinking that always being connected is going to make us feel less alone. But we're at risk, because actually it's the opposite that's true. If we're not able to be alone, we're going to be more lonely. And if we don't teach our children to be alone, they're only going to know how to be lonely."[41]

Turkle's research illuminates a truth about life with God as well. If we don't cultivate solitude and silence, we won't have a sense of self to share with God. We won't know what's really inside us or be able to identify the fears, joys, and struggles that ought to fill our prayers. And if we are never alone with God, it is unlikely that we will come to recognize the presence of God in others.

 READ MORE Luke 5:12–16; Psalm 139:1–24

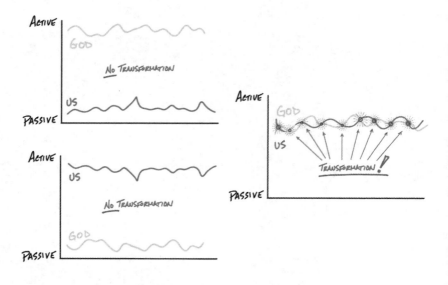

IF JESUS WAS SERIOUS...
THEN WE MUST AVOID OVER-
EMPHASIZING ACTIVITY OR
PASSIVITY.

I RECENTLY HEARD an interview with a Christian who has
been active in politics for decades, but has now come to a place
of deep concern. As a younger man, he called Christians to political engagement. He believed Christians would let their faith
shape their politics, but he now confesses the opposite has happened. His experience has shown that most people start with a

political ideology and then their "faith is twisted into a pretzel in order to fit into that ideology."

What caught my attention in the interview, however, was not the man's remarks about politics, but rather his disillusionment with faith. "Frankly, there are fewer transformed lives than I thought there would be. . . . The capacity for faith to alter the human heart and the affections of the heart is less than I anticipated."[42]

I could hear the disappointment in his voice. It's a tone I've heard in the voices of many Christians over the years—both young and old, leaders and laity, conservative and progressive. The lack of transformation causes many to blame Christianity itself, but I'm convinced the real problem isn't our faith but instead how it is practiced. The shape it takes in many communities simply doesn't create an environment for growth and transformation.

In some places the faith is all about activity. People assume the more we do *for* God the more we'll be transformed. (I suspect this was the default posture of the Christian political activists encountered by the man being interviewed.) Other communities present a faith of passivity. Works diminish God's grace, they argue, so it's best to simply wait for God to miraculously intervene in your life and character. In both types of communities, transformation is unlikely to occur, leading to the disillusionment we currently see.

Eugene Peterson wrote that "prayer takes place in the middle voice."[43] It's a helpful metaphor that applies to faith broadly and not merely to prayer. In Greek the active voice is employed for the person taking action, and the passive voice for the one being acted upon. These align with the two common approaches to faith—activity and passivity.

The middle voice is different. It's used when a group of people act upon one another. As Peterson says, "We neither manipulate God (active voice) nor are manipulated by God (passive voice). We are involved in the action and participate in its results but do not control or define it (middle voice)."[44]

The middle voice best describes what Christian prayer looks like, and why it is an essential practice for those who seek real growth and transformation. Prayer is not merely how we express ourselves to God, and it's not how we passively wait for God to do something in us. Instead, true prayer is communion and cooperation *with* God. It's the mysterious push and pull, give and take, action and reaction of Creator and creature as we act upon each other. The gracious privilege of relating to God in this way is granted only to us because we alone have been made in His image.

 READ MORE **Philippians 2:12–13; 2 Peter 1:3–11**

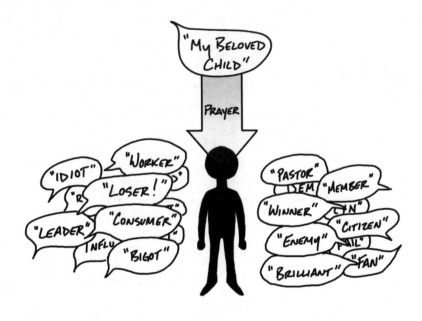

52 IF JESUS WAS SERIOUS...
THEN PRAYER TRANSFORMS OUR
FEAR INTO LOVE.

AS JESUS PRAYED TO HIS FATHER in Gethsemane, Luke describes Him as being in "agony." The fear and pain was so intense "his sweat became like great drops of blood falling to the ground" (Luke 22:44). This is not the image of a serene Messiah accepting His fate, but of an agonized man wrestling with the darkest evil our world can dispense.

But through prayer, Luke says, Jesus was strengthened. The power given to Him, however, was not like the world's power. When the soldiers arrived to arrest Him, His disciples were terrified and in their fear some fled and others attacked. Peter drew a sword and severed the ear of one of the men. This is what the world's power looks like. It fights. It attacks. It kills.

The strength Jesus was given through communion with His Father was different. Displaying a power not of this world, He knelt to the ground, picked up the severed ear of His enemy, and healed him. "Put your sword back," He told Peter. "For all who take the sword will perish by the sword" (Matt. 26:52). Through prayer Jesus' fear had been transformed into faith. His faith gave Him strength. And this strength was revealed in love.

This same transformation of fear into unworldly strength is available to us and to all who follow Christ. Consider the story of Praying Jacob, a slave who lived in Maryland before the Civil War. It was his habit to stop his work periodically in the fields to pray. This practice gave Jacob his nickname, and it also enraged his owner—a cruel and terrible man named Saunders. One day Saunders came up to Jacob while he was praying and put a gun to his head. He ordered him to stop praying and get back to work.

Jacob finished his prayers and invited Saunders to pull the trigger. "Your loss will be my gain," he said. "I have a soul and a body; the body belongs to you, but my soul belongs to Jesus." Saunders was so shaken by Jacob's strength and unnatural lack of fear that he never touched him again.

Praying Jacob's serenity came from the assurance of his identity. He knew he belonged to Jesus, and nothing would ever remove him from His hand. Not even death. This was the same faith Jesus displayed in the garden and throughout

His journey to the grave. He knew He belonged to His Father. Despite the betrayal and abandonment of His friends. Despite the injustice of the authorities. Despite the mocking and torture of the Romans. Despite the insults and ridicule hurled at Him from the crowds. Jesus still found the strength to love because He knew who He was and whose He was.

Like Jesus and Praying Jacob, if we learn to listen to the voice of God in prayer, our pain can also be transformed into love. As Henri Nouwen said, "You can deal with an enormous amount of success as well as enormous amount of failure without losing your identity, because your identity is that you are the beloved. . . . Long before you were rejected by some person or praised by somebody else—that voice has been there always. 'I have loved you with an everlasting love.' That love is there before you were born and will be there after you die."[45]

 READ MORE Luke 22:39–46; Matthew 26:47–56

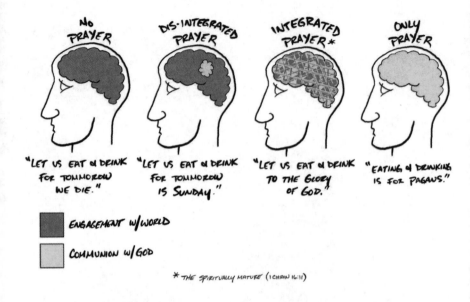

NO PRAYER

DIS-INTEGRATED PRAYER

INTEGRATED PRAYER *

ONLY PRAYER

"LET US EAT & DRINK FOR TOMMOROW WE DIE."

"LET US EAT & DRINK FOR TOMMOROW IS SUNDAY."

"LET US EAT & DRINK TO THE GLORY OF GOD."

"EATING & DRINKING IS FOR PAGANS."

⬛ ENGAGEMENT w/ WORLD

⬜ COMMUNION w/ GOD

*THE SPIRITUALLY MATURE (1 CHRON 16:11)

53 IF JESUS WAS SERIOUS... THEN WE WILL SEE GOD EVEN AMID DARKNESS.

JESUS' ENEMIES SAW HIM teaching and healing in the temple each day, but they waited until nightfall to arrest Him in a secluded place because they knew their actions were unjust and unwarranted. Their plot to capture Jesus was contrary to God's law and they had no evidence to legally justify executing Him. That's why, when the soldiers arrived in the garden with swords and clubs, Jesus said, "This is your hour, and the power of darkness" (Luke 22:53).

And yet Jesus saw more than evil at work that night. He also saw the providence of God. He rebuked His disciples for responding with fear and violence. Jesus told them to put away their weapons. "Do you think I cannot appeal to my Father, and he will at once send me more than twelve legions of angels? But how then should the Scriptures be fulfilled?" (Matt. 26:53–54). Somehow, amid the injustice and darkness unfolding in the garden that night, Jesus recognized what C. S. Lewis called "a deeper magic." God's plan, foretold in Scripture, was being accomplished. What His enemies intended for evil, God was simultaneously using to accomplish good.

For Jesus, and those who share His mind, things are not so easily separated into definite categories of *good* and *evil*, *sacred* and *secular*, or *Christian* and *non-Christian*. The very thing we assume to be evil or unrighteous may be an unwitting instrument of God. And those parts of the world we think to be insignificant to Christ are often precisely where He may be found. God's ever-present "deeper magic" means we must discern layers of meaning and see beyond the surface. This capacity is the mark of a mature Christian.

The immature still see the world, their life, and their faith as one dimensional and comprised of dis-integrated components. They still see Sunday as sacred but Monday as secular. They call the church holy and the pub profane. They think prayer is a religious activity and golf is a recreational one. To those with a dis-integrated vision, everything has a single meaning or identity. There is no mystery, no deeper magic. For a Christian who thinks this way, prayer will forever remain an isolated category or religious behavior. Communion with God will never permeate their life or transform their world.

The move toward an integrated vision of the world, like the one Jesus displayed on the night of His arrest, requires breaking open the prayer category in our imagination and allowing it to seep into every part of our life. As we carry our communion with God into everything we do and everywhere we go, we will begin to see those places and activities differently. We will perceive with eyes of faith the deeper layers, mysteries, and magic that are at work. And even in the hours when darkness reigns, we will still recognize the presence of the One who promised to never leave us.

 READ MORE Isaiah 43:1–7; Matthew 26:47–56

NOTES

1. "Church Priorities for 2005 Vary Considerably," Barna Group, February 14, 2005, https://www.barna.com/research/church-priorities-for-2005-vary -considerably/.

2. Abraham Joshua Heschel, *Moral Grandeur and Spiritual Audacity: Essays Edited by Susannah Heschel* (New York: Farrar, Straus & Giroux, 1996), 107.

3. *Westminster Confession of Faith* 7:1.

4. Richard J. Foster, *Prayer: Finding the Heart's True Home* (New York: HarperOne, 1992), 8.

5. St. Augustine of Hippo, *The Letters of St. Augustine: Annotated Edition*, John George Cunningham, trans. (Altenmünster, Germany: Jazzybee Verlag, 2015), 260.

6. "5 Reasons Millennials Stay Connected to Church," Barna Group, September 17, 2013, https://www.barna.com/research/5-reasons -millennials-stay-connected-to-church/.

7. Madam Guyon, *Experiencing the Depths of Jesus Christ* (Goleta, CA: Chris-tian Books, 1975), 47.

8. C. S. Lewis, *The Joyful Christian* (United Kingdom: Scribner, 1996), 101.

9. Lewis, *The Joyful Christian*, 102.

10. Jurjen Beumer, *Henri Nouwen: A Restless Seeking for God* (Chestnut Ridge, NY: Crossroad Publishing, 1997), 44.

11. Quoted in C. S. Lewis, *Letters to Malcolm: Chiefly on Prayer* (United Kingdom: G. Bles, 1964), 33.

12. Henri Nouwen, "Moving from Solitude to Community to Ministry," *Leadership Journal*, Spring 1995, 83.

13. Quoted in C. S. Lewis, *Letters to Malcolm*, 36.

14. Robert Harrison, ed., Johanna van Gogh-Bonger, trans., *The Complete Letters of Vincent van Gogh* (New York: Bulfinch Press, 1991), Letter 248.

15. John Dalrymple, *Simple Prayer* (Wilmington, DE: Michael Glazier, 1984), 13.

16. Quoted in Chuck Swindoll, *So, You Want to Be Like Christ?: Eight Essentials to Get You There* (Nashville: Thomas Nelson, 2005), 61–62.

17. *The Practice of the Presence of God: Being Conversation and Letters of Nicolas Herman of Lorraine*, 5th ed. (London: James Nisbet & Co., Limited, 1904), 7.

18. Sheldon Cheney, *Men Who Have Walked with God* (Whitefish, MT: Kessinger Publishing, 1997), 303.

19. "Brother Lawrence: Practitioner of God's Presence," *Christian History*, https://www.christianitytoday.com/history/people/innertravelers /brother-lawrence.html.

20. Brother Lawrence (Nicholas Herman), *The Practice of the Presence of God* (Grand Rapids: Baker Publishing Group), 1967, Fifth Letter.

21. Thomas R. Kelly, *A Testament of Devotion* (New York: HarperCollins, 1996), 9.

22. Dallas Willard, quoted in Bill Gaultiere, "Dallas Willard's Definitions," *Soul Shepherding*, https://www.soulshepherding.org/dallas-willards-definitions.

23. Ibid.

24. T. W. Wilson, quoted in Harold Myra and Marshall Shelley, *The Leadership Secrets of Billy Graham* (Grand Rapids, MI: Zondervan, 2005), 293.

25. Blaise Pascal, quoted in Richard J. Foster, *Prayer: Finding the Heart's True Home* (New York: HarperOne, 1992), 229.

26. Ole Hallesby, *Prayer* (London: Hodder & Stoughton, 1963), 117.

27. Dallas Willard, *The Divine Conspiracy: Rediscovering Our Hidden Life In God* (New York: HarperOne, 2009), 208.

28. Keith Beasley-Topliffe, ed. *Writings of Evelyn Underhill* (Nashville: Upper Room Books), 2017.

29. C. S. Lewis, *Letters to Malcolm, Chiefly on Prayer* (New York: HarperOne, 2017), 11.

30. *The Book of Common Prayer* (Huntington Beach, CA: Anglican Liturgy Press, 2019), 130.

31. Henri Nouwen, quoted in Tony Jones, *The Sacred Way* (Grand Rapids, MI: Zondervan: 2005), 32.

32. Christopher Chabris and Daniel Simons, "The Invisible Gorilla," http://www.theinvisiblegorilla.com.

33. Paul F. Bradshaw, *Early Christian Worship: A Basic Introduction to Ideas and Practice* (Collegeville, MN: Liturgical Press, 1996), 45.

34. Paraphrased from Søren Kierkegaard, Journalen JJ:167 (1843), Søren Kierkegaards Skrifter (Copenhagen: Søren Kierkegaard Research Center, 1997), 306.

35. C. S. Lewis, quoted in Wayne Martindale, Jerry Rood, and Linda Washington, eds., *The Soul of C. S. Lewis: A Meditative Journey through Twenty-Six of His Best-Loved Writings* (Wheaton, IL: Tyndale House Publishers, 2010), 125.

36. Mary DeMuth, quoted in Kate Shellnutt, "1 in 10 Young Protestants Have Left a Church over Abuse," christianitytoday.com, May 21, 2019, http://www.christianitytoday.com/news/2019/may/lifeway-protestant-abuse-survey-young-christians-leave-chur.html.

37. Richard J. Foster, *Prayer: Finding the Heart's True Home*, 10th Anniversary Edition (New York: HarperOne, 2009), 14.

38. Wayne Martindale and Jerry Root, *The Quotable Lewis* (Wheaton, IL: Tyndale House Publishers, 1989), 548.

39. This quote has been variously attributed to John Stuart Mill and Edmund Burke; the actual author remains unknown.

40. "2018 Cigna U.S. Loneliness Index," www.multivu.com/players/English/8294451-cigna-us-loneliness-survey/docs/IndexReport_1524069371598-173525450.pdf.

41. Sherry Turkle, "Connected, but Alone?," TED 2012, https://www.ted.com/talks/sherry_turkle_connected_but_alone/transcript?language=en.

42. Peter Wehner, "Peter Wehner on Trump, Impeachment, and the Limits of Faith to Overcome Political Ideology," *The Long Game* podcast, https://podcasts.apple.com/us/podcast/peter-wehner-on-trump-impeachment-limits-faith-to-overcome/id1248994688?i=1000441130129.

43. Eugene H. Peterson, *The Contemplative Pastor: Returning to the Art of Spiritual Direction* (Carol Stream, IL: Christianity Today, 1989), 110.

44. Peterson, *The Contemplative Pastor*, 111.

45. Henri Nouwen, "From Solitude to Community to Ministry," Christianity Today, April 1, 1995, https://www.christianitytoday.com/pastors/1995/spring/5l280.html.

If Jesus was serious . . . then why don't we take Him more seriously?

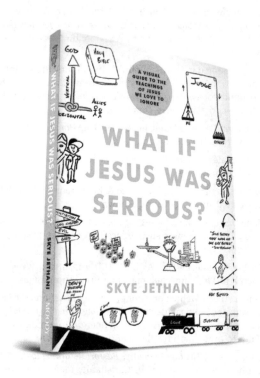